For my parents,
Bob Lloyd Carter and
Beverly Ann Averett Carter

Working

with

Computer

Type

A RotoVision Book
Published and Distributed by RotoVision SA
Route Suisse 9
1295 Mies
Switzerland

Tel   41 (22) 775 30 55
Fax   41 (22) 755 40 72

Distributed to the trade in the United States by

Watson Guptill Publications
1515 Broadway
New York, New York 10036

ISBN 2-88046-230-4

Book design by Rob Carter and Matt Woolman

Production and separations in Singapore by

ProVision Pte. Ltd.
Tel   65 334 7720
Fax   65 334 7721

Working with Computer Type

Computer Type

**Books
Magazines
Newsletters**

ROTOVISION

Contents

Desktop technology has forever changed the graphic design profession. User-friendly page composition programs make it possible for anyone with a desktop computer to make books, brochures, pamphlets, and any number of other materials. Widely available are programmed formats that aid the novice in preparing such materials. Thus, many jobs that once required a hired graphic designer are now accomplished in-house by non-designers. As cost effective as home grown graphic design is, it is often substandard; for simply having access to high-tech tools is not a replacement for the knowledge required to use them appropriately. A twenty-minute page-layout tutorial for the computer will never replace a professional graphic designer's trained eye, education, and experience. This is not to say that low-end graphic design is not of value; clearly it has a valid place in the expansive world of visual communication. Non-designers, hobbiests, and office staff assigned graphic design tasks should be encouraged to learn as much as possible about typography and design so they may use their computers and software more effectively. But high-end graphic design will undoubtedly continue in the domain of the professional designer.

Until the mid-1980s, a graphic designer worked hand-in-hand with a craftsman called a compositor who was specifically trained to compose type. Upon the completion of a layout, the designer would send a typewritten manuscript marked with copyfitting specifications to this expert for typesetting. The compositor would then return to the designer a set of proofs or galleys that hopefully matched exactly the designer's specifications. If changes were needed, the proofs were returned to the compositor for alterations. When type proofs met the expectations of the designer, they were pasted onto mechanicals, which were then sent to the printer. While this process was quite tedious, it led to excellent results.

Graphic designers have traditionally been connoisseurs of fine typography, but until recently, they have rarely, if ever, set their own type. The advent of desktop publishing has changed the original graphic design process, resulting in a shift of responsibilities. Designers now often wear several hats, including those of designer *and* typesetter. This shift has caught many by surprise – almost overnight, traditional typesetting tools and skills have been replaced with new ones. Designers now wishing to make typographic refinements in spacing, kerning, and ragging must do so by themselves at the desktop.

Changes in typographic technology have traditionally brought about changes in the appearance of type. When metal type was the exclusive means for setting type, the spacing of letters was restricted by the physical shape of the type block itself. With the development of phototype in the 1960s, however, designers were for the first time able to make letters touch and overlap. Suddenly, books, magazines, and other publications were characterized by tight, even touching letters, particularly in headlines. The use of computers has had an amazingly profound effect upon the appearance of type. For the professional graphic designer and novice alike, technology has become a double-edged sword. Digital type, generated by pixels, enables great flexibility. Amazing visual effects which may or may not improve or enhance the intended message can be achieved using current computer software. On one hand, classical letterforms can be wildly and irresponsibly distorted from their original designs, violating the integrity of the type designer's work; on the other hand, the visual nuances in type can be adjusted for improved typographic readability and quality. Perhaps the best computer-aided typographic design is that in which the computer is not visually apparent, where its role in the design process remains transparent. Perhaps the worst work is that which reeks – without regard for the message's content – of the gimmicks and tricks made available by computer software.

Another factor affecting typographic practice today is the new high-tech work station. For the most part, T-squares, triangles, technical pens, and drawing boards have been replaced by a mouse and computer screen. Designers must adjust their typographic sensitivities to this non-tactile, contained environment. More than ever, the nuances of type as it appears on the lumi-nescent computer screen must be understood for meaningful and effective practice. Designers must knowingly guide the computer rather than be guided by it. The computer is only a tool – albeit a powerful one – to be used as a facilitator in the design process. Knowing its limitations and strengths in this process is crucial.

This book is written under the premise that book and magazine design as it was tradition-ally practiced demands continuous reference and acknowledgement; indeed, it should be held in high regard. Standards of book design as it has evolved over the centuries should be studied and considered before blind departures into uncharted, experimental terrain. With a solid respect and understanding of normative standards, experimentation can extend the practice of book design and enrich the reading experience.

The examples presented in this book represent the work of noted designers throughout the world, and they cover a wide spectrum, from purely functional and traditional designs to the most radical of experiments. Going far beyond the typical design annual, each example is thoroughly discussed, with focus upon the essence of the design, visual organization and structure, and the specific use of typefaces. In a sense, the book doubles as a type specimen book. Effective typographic practice is based upon a need to broadly understand typefaces and their potential for communication and expression within the context of specific mes-sages. This book helps to fulfill that need. The collection of examples as a whole provides an invaluable handbook of typographic possibili-ties. For the professional designer, this book observes a wide range of sophisticated type treatments. For the non-designer and aspiring desktop publisher, it covers typographic basics and helps to clarify the often bewildering world of typography. Professional designers, art direc-tors, students, and desktop publishers will find this source informative, inspiring, and useful.

duction

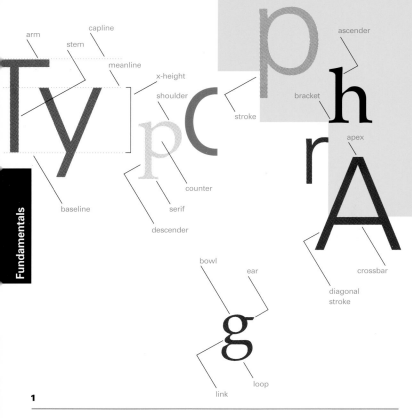

1

arm
capline
stem
meanline
x-height
shoulder
stroke
baseline
serif
descender
counter
ascender
bracket
apex
crossbar
diagonal stroke
bowl
ear
link
loop

g

B B B B B B B

eye

2

Some things never change, and in the typographic realm, principles upon which sound practice rely have remained essentially the same for centuries. These principles have over time developed in response to the way in which we read – the way in which we visually perceive the letters and words on a page. Working effectively with computer type (or working with type using any tool for that matter) requires a solid knowledge of these typographic fundamentals. The following pages provide the reader with the basic vocabulary needed for informed practice, and a fuller understanding and appreciation of the case studies presented within this book.

The anatomy of type
The colorful terms used to describe type are not unlike the terms used to describe the parts of our own bodies. Letters have arms, legs, eyes, spines, and a few other parts such as tails and stems, that we, fortunately do not possess. These are the parts that have historically been used to construct letterforms. Learning this vocabulary can help the designer gain appreciation for the complexity of our alphabet, which at first glance appears very simple (fig. **1**). The structure of letters within the alphabet remains constant regardless of typeface. An uppercase *B*, for example, consists of one vertical and two curved strokes. These parts, however, may be expressed very differently from typeface to typeface (fig. **2**).

Type classification
An inexhaustible variety of type styles is available for use today, and many attempts to classify these into logical groupings have fallen short due to the overlapping visual traits of typefaces. A flawless classification system does not exist; however, a general system based on the historical development of typefaces is used widely. This delineation breaks down typefaces into the following groups: Old Style, Transitional, Modern, Slab Serif (also called Egyptian), Sans Serif, and Display (fig. **3**).

The typographic font
In desktop publishing, the terms typeface and font are often used synonymously; however, a typeface is the design of characters unified by consistent visual properties, while a font is the complete set of characters in any one design, size, or style of type. These characters include but are not limited to upper- and lower-case letters, numerals, small capitals, fractions, ligatures (two or more characters linked together into a single unit), punctuation, mathematical

Old Style characteristics:
Medium stroke contrast
Slanted stress
Oblique, bracketed serifs
Medium overall weight

Transitional characteristics:
Medium to high stroke contrast
Nearly vertical stress
Sharp, bracketed serifs
Slightly slanted serifs

Modern characteristics:
High stroke contrast
Vertical stress
Thin serifs
Serifs sometimes unbracketed

Egyptian characteristics:
Little stroke contrast
Little or no stress
Thick, square serifs
Large x-height

Sans serif characteristics:
Some stroke contrast
Nearly vertical stress
Squarish curved strokes
Lower case *g* has open tail

Display typefaces do not possess a fixed number of characteristics.

Old Style

Transitional

Modern

Slab serif

Sans serif

Display

k
leg
foot

j
tail

spine

3

O

abcdefghijklmnopqrstuvwxyz
ABCDEFGHIJKLMNOPQRSTUVWXYZ&
ABCDEFGHIJKLMNOPQRSTUVWXYZ&
(.,;:,!?""''‹›~‵‵\`´´´‵˘˙ˆˇ ~'''«»‹›- – —)
1234567890 1234567890 ($^{1234567890}/_{1234567890}$)
¼⅓½⅔¾⅝⅞%‰ [+√π=≠±≤≥÷∞º]
fffiflffiffflŒßæœ $£§¢
ÂÅÁÇÍÎÏØÓÒÔÚ áéíóúåäëïöüàèìòùâêîô
¶‡†•⋆∧ ©™@

4

signs, accents, monetary symbols, and miscellaneous dingbats (assorted ornaments or fleurons designed for use in a font). Supplementing some desktop fonts are expert sets, which include characters such as small caps, a good selection of ligatures, fractions, and nonaligning figures. Minion Regular provides an excellent example of a font and its attendant expert set (fig. **4**).

The type family
A type family is a group of typefaces bound together by similar visual characteristics. Members of a family (typefaces) resemble one another, but also have their own unique visual traits. Typefaces within families consist of different weights and widths. Some type families consist of many members; others are composed of just a few. Extended families such as Stone include both serif and sans serif variations (fig. **5**).

Typographic measurement
The two primary units of measure in typography are the pica and the point. There are approximately six picas or 72 points to an inch; there are twelve points to a pica (fig. **6**). Points are used to specify the size of type, which includes the cap height of letters, plus a small interval of space above and below the letters. Typefaces of the same size may in fact appear different in size, depending on the size of the x-height. At the same size, letters with large x-heights appear larger than letters with smaller x-heights. Points are also used to measure the distance between lines; picas are used to measure the lengths of lines. The unit, a relative measure determined by dividing the em (which is the square of the type size), is used to reduce or increase the amount of space between letters, a process called tracking. Adjusting the awkward space between two letters to create consistency within words is called kerning.

The typographic grid
A typographic grid is used to aid the designer in organizing typographic and pictorial elements on a page and establishing unity among all of the parts of a design. Grids vary in complexity and configuration depending upon the nature of the information needing accommodation, and the physical properties of the typographic elements. Standard typographic grids possess flow lines, grid modules, text columns, column intervals, and margins (fig. **7**).

Stone Serif

Regular
Regular Italic
Semibold
Semibold Italic
Bold
Bold Italic

Stone Sans

Regular
Regular Italic
Semibold
Semibold Italic
Bold
Bold Italic

5

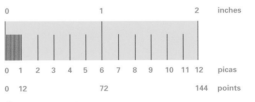

| 0 | | 1 | | 2 | inches |

| 0 | 1 | 2 | 3 | 4 | 5 | 6 | 7 | 8 | 9 | 10 | 11 | 12 | picas |
| 0 | 12 | | | | | 72 | | | | | | 144 | points |

6 picas = 1 inch
12 points = 1 pica
72 points = 1 inch

6

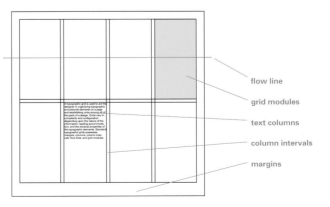

flow line

grid modules

text columns

column intervals

margins

7

Bembo

Baskerville

Bodoni

Century Expanded

Garamond

Franklin Gothic

Frutiger

Futura

Gill Sans

Helvetica

8

8/9
Line spacing ensures that the reader is not distracted by lines of type that visually run together. With inadequate space between lines, the eye struggles to distinguish one line from the next. Where lines are too widely spaced, the reader has trouble locating the next line. For optimum sizes of text type (8-11 point), one to four points of line

8/10
Line spacing ensures that the reader is not distracted by lines of type that visually run together. With inadequate space between lines, the eye struggles to distinguish one line from the next. Where lines are too widely spaced, the reader has trouble locating the next line. For optimum sizes of text type (8-11

8/11
Line spacing ensures that the reader is not distracted by lines of type that visually run together. With inadequate space between lines, the eye struggles to distinguish one line from the next. Where lines are too widely spaced, the reader has trouble locating the next line. For

8/12
Line spacing ensures that the reader is not distracted by lines of type that visually run together. With inadequate space between lines, the eye struggles to distinguish one line from the next. Where lines are too widely spaced, the reader has trouble locating the next line. For

10

Overly long or short lines of type also tire the reader, and destroy a pleasant reading rhythm. Long lines are burdensome and tedious, whereas short lines cause choppy eye movements. Paying attention to the number of characters per line is a key in

Legibility

If the goal when working with type is to make it more readable, then heeding established legibility guidelines is of utmost importance. Departure from these "rules" should be attempted only after a designer is totally familiarized with them, and when content lends itself to expressive interpretation. Legibility represents those visual attributes in typography that make type readable.

Choosing typefaces
The first step in making type legible is to choose text typefaces that are open and well proportioned, typefaces that exhibit the regularity of classical serif faces such as Baskerville, Bembo, Bodoni, Garamond; and the sans serif faces Franklin Gothic, Frutiger, and Gill Sans (fig. **8**). Typefaces with visual quirks, stylistic affectations, and irregularities among characters are less legible. Typefaces such as these may be fine, however, when used as display type.

Type size, line length, and line spacing
Text that flows naturally when read is achieved when a harmonious relationship exists between type size, line length, and the spaces between lines of type (line spacing or leading). Even well-designed typefaces suffer from legibility impairment when just one of these aspects is out of balance. An adjustment to one of these factors usually requires an adjustment to one or more of the others.

Continuous text type that is too large or too small easily tires the reader. Optimum sizes for text type are between 8 and 11 points. Also, typefaces with a relatively large x-height improve readability.

Overly long or short lines of type also tire the reader and destroy a pleasant reading rhythm. Long lines are burdensome and tedious, whereas short lines cause choppy eye movements. Paying attention to the number of characters per line is a key in determining appropriate line lengths. It is generally agreed that lines of type consisting of a maximum of sixty or seventy characters promote readability (fig. **9**).

Line spacing ensures that the reader is not distracted by lines of type that visually run together. Without adequate space between lines, the eye struggles to distinguish one line from the next. Where lines are too widely spaced, the reader has trouble locating the next

Overly long or short lines of type also tire the reader, and destroy a pleasant reading rhythm. Long lines are burdensome and tedious, whereas short lines cause choppy eye movements. Paying attention to the number of characters per line is a key in determining appropriate line lengths. It is

9

line. For optimum sizes of text type (8-11 points), one to four points of line spacing can help the reader easily discern each line, thus improving readability (fig. **10**).

Letter spacing
A number of factors determines correct letter spacing, including the typeface used, and the size and weight of the type. Consistent letter spacing provides an even typographic "color," a term referring to the texture and overall lightness or darkness of text. Consistent and even color is an attribute that enhances readability. Tighter letter spacing darkens the text, as in this sentence. Looser letter spacing lightens the text. Pushed to either extreme, text becomes less readable. The chosen effect can enliven a page and enhance communication.

Word spacing
Word spacing should be proportionally adjusted to letter spacing so that letters flow gracefully and rhythmically into words, and words into lines. Too much word spacing destroys the even texture desired in text and causes words to become disjointed, as in this sentence. Toolittlewordspacing causeswordstobumpintooneanother. Either condition is hard on the reader.

Weight
The overall heaviness or lightness of the strokes composing type can affect readability. For typefaces that are too heavy, counters fill in and disappear. Typefaces that are too light are not easily distinguished from their background. Typefaces of contrasting weight are effectively used to create emphasis within text.

Width
Narrow typefaces are effectively used where there is an abundance of text, and space must be preserved. But readability is diminished when letters are too narrow (condensed) or too wide (expanded). Condensed letters fit nicely into narrow columns.

Italics
Italic and oblique type should be used with prudence, for large amounts of slanted characters set into text impede reading. Italics are best suited to create emphasis within text rather than to function as text.

Capitals versus lower-case
TEXT SET IN ALL CAPITAL LETTERS NOT ONLY CONSUMES MORE SPACE THAN TEXT SET IN LOWER-CASE, IT SEVERELY RETARDS THE READING PROCESS. LOWER-CASE LETTERS IMBUE TEXT WITH VISUAL CUES CREATED BY AN ABUNDANCE OF LETTER SHAPES, ASCENDERS, DESCENDERS, AND IRREGULAR WORD SHAPES. TEXT SET IN ALL CAPITALS IS VOID OF THESE CUES, FOR IT LACKS THIS VISUAL VARIETY.

Serif versus sans serif
Because of the horizontal flow created by serifs, it was thought at one time that serif typefaces were more readable than sans serif typefaces. Legibility research, however, reveals little difference between them. Sensitive letter spacing is a more important consideration.

Justified versus unjustified
Text can be aligned in five different ways: flush left, ragged right; flush right, ragged left; justified; centered; asymmetrically.

Flush left, ragged right text produces very even letter and word spacing, and because lines of type terminate at different points, the reader is able to easily locate each new line. This is perhaps the most legible means of aligning text.

Flush right, ragged left alignments work against the reader by making it difficult to find each new line. This method is suitable for small amounts of text, but is not recommended for large amounts.

Justified text (text aligned both left and right) can be very readable if the designer ensures that the spacing between letters and words is consistent, and that awkward gaps called "rivers" do not interrupt the flow of the text. Desktop publishing software enables the designer to fine tune the spacing.

Centered alignments give the text a very formal appearance and are fine when used minimally. But setting large amounts of text in this way should be avoided.

Asymmetrical alignments are used when the designer wishes to

break the text down into logical "thought units,"

or to give the page a more expressive appearance. Obviously, setting large amounts of text in this manner

will tire the reader.

When books are published as a series, it is the designer's task to visually tie the volumes together as a unified family. *A History of Western Society* is an excellent example of a cohesively designed series of covers, a homogenous mixture of type and image. Drama is established in the covers with the use of full-bleed portraits cropped from paintings created during the specific periods covered in the books. The use of human portraits from different times emphasizes the subject of social history. A flexible typographic system accommodates variations in cover information, such as the subtitles that change from book to book. Harold Burch, the designer of the covers, effectively balances visual similarities and differences for a spirited series.

Containing the title type within boxed spaces was inspired by a trip to Amsterdam, where this stylistic tendency is prevalent. Essentially, each box is a zone to which specific title information is assigned. Units composing the title appear in exactly the same location from cover to cover for unity. The main title, which in each cover remains identical except for color, is composed of three interlocking rectangles prominently positioned in the upper part of the space. The subtitles are constructed by distributing the information in stacked rectangles in the bottom left section. The number of rectangles varies depending on subtitle lengths.

The placement of these elements is a deliberate attempt to logically direct the reader's eye from one part of the cover to another. Upon seeing a cover, the reader focuses first upon the dominant image. The eye then travels to the main title (we are accustomed to reading from top to bottom and left to right). The subtitle is last to be read. This is a three-tiered hierarchy composed of dominant, subdominant, and subordinate features (see diagram below).

McKay Hill Buckler

A *History of*
WESTERN SOCIETY 5th Edition

SINCE 1400

Text covers from the *History of Western Society,* Fifth Edition, series by John P. McKay, Bennett D. Hill, and John Buckler. Copyright © 1991 by Houghten Mifflin Company. Reprinted with permission.

While the title typography appears relatively simple, it is built upon a rather complex visual scheme. The title, *A History of Western Society,* is divided into two parts. *A History of,* set in letter spaced Century Old Style Italics, is printed in red on a solid box whose color is pulled from the cover image. This type-face represents the "history" aspect of the books. *Western Society* is set in all-capitals Gill Sans and is reversed from the cover image to appear as white. This typeface implies a current interpretation of history. The box for this element is framed by a ruled line, creating a window through which the underlying image can be seen. This adds a rich three-dimensionality to the cover.

Corresponding to the covers, spines of the books are simi-larly compartmentalized for unity (below).

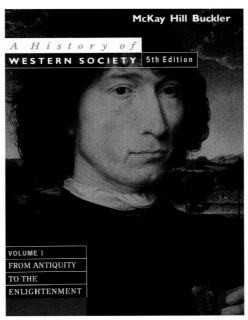

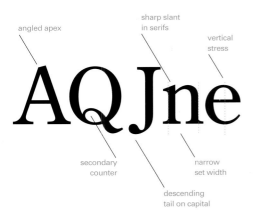

angled apex

sharp slant in serifs

vertical stress

secondary counter

narrow set width

descending tail on capital

Century Old Style is a highly readable member of the Century family, which includes Century Roman, cut in 1894 by L.B. Benton and T.L. DeVinne, and Century Schoolbook, designed in 1915 by Morris F. Benton. Because of the legibility and practicality of these types, they continue in popularity.

When placing type within boxes, be careful not to crowd letters so close to the edges as to create a disturb-ing visual tension (top). Let the type breathe by surround-ing it with adequate spatial

intervals that harmonize with letter and word spacing (middle). Aligning type to the edge of a box is a viable alter-native that retains typograph-ic integrity (bottom).

TYPE IN A BOX

TYPE IN A BOX

TYPE IN A BOX

This guide to San Francisco architecture provides easy access to abundant and complex information. Its geographical organization, clean and functional page design, and typographical simplicity enable readers to quickly find buildings, parks, and public artworks in the Bay area. Helvetica Condensed in three weights (Regular, Bold, and Black) facilitates an economic use of space and visual distinction between heads, subheads, and text. The typeface's high character count, distinctive visual quality, and readability qualify it as an excellent choice for this guide. Despite the large amount of information contained within the book, its spacious appearance and succinct visual organization empower the reader with pleasant and unencumbered reading.

The purpose of this guidebook is to lead the reader through information as clearly and easily as possible. It is appropriate that Helvetica Condensed was chosen for this job, for its simplicity of form and architectural qualities match the content of the book. When you are choosing a typeface for a given task, choose one that has a visual affinity to the subject matter at hand. Compare Helvetica Condensed (top) with two other typefaces whose visual qualities suggest other possible uses. Journal (middle), and Zephyr Script (bottom).

A sculptural, contemporary version of the classical skyscraper with the corners visually strengthened by paired columns. Panels of precast bosses attempt to overcome the blankness of the typical office tower; expanses of glass permit a view into the banking hall. At

A sculptural, contemporary version of the classical skyscraper with the corners visually strengthened by paired columns. Panels of precast bosses attempt to overcome the blankness of the typical

A sculptural, contemporary version of the classical skyscraper with the corners visually strengthened by paired columns. Panels of precast bosses attempt to overcome the blankness of the typical office tower; expanses of glass permit a view into the banking hall.

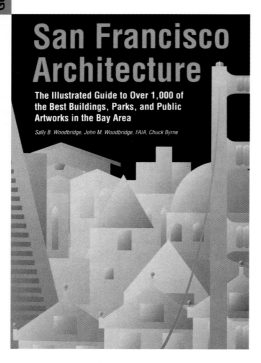

The title for *San Francisco Architecture* is designed for impact and readability. Though "big" is not always better, here the large scale of the title immediately introduces a potential buyer to the book.

This book tours architectural landmarks by listing them by geographical location. Because hundreds of sites are described, it is critical that the reader is capable of easily distinguishing between them. Individual site listings are set in 9/11 Helvetica Condensed throughout, with names listed in Black, addresses in Bold Italic, and descriptions of sites in Regular. Using the same size of type throughout but changing the weight and using italics for emphasis is an effective, simple, and visually economic way to identify the various parts of the information (top). Other typographic possibilities exist, but using too many typographic variations simultaneously such as size, style, italics, and weight can overly complicate the information, thus making it difficult to read (bottom). Much like a child in a candy shop, a novice typographer is faced with an endless supply of goodies. Learning to keep things simple requires restraint, training, and practice.

44. San Francisco Art Institute
1926, Bakewell & Brown;
add. 1970, Paffard Keatinge Clay
800 Chestnut St.
Two versions of exposed concrete, each highly successful in its own way. The older building is a stripped down but

44. SAN FRANCISCO ART INSTITUTE
1926, Bakewell & Brown;
add. 1970, Paffard Keatinge Clay
800 Chestnut St.
Two versions of exposed concrete, each highly successful in its own way. The older building is a

1. Union Square
1850
Geary to Post, Powell to Stockton Sts.

2. St. Francis Hotel
1904-07, 1913, Bliss & Faville
Hotel Tower, 1972, William Pereira
301-45 Powell St.

Gutted in the 1906 fire, the hotel was restored and enlarged by the first architects. In 1913 an addition on the Post Street end altered its symmetrical E shape. Typical of the Renaissance Revival style then in vogue, the building is treated like a stretched Italian palazzo with an ornate cornice and a ground floor arcade. Wide, rusticated bands running up the mid-section tie the top and bottom together. The ground floor arcade extends its influence across the sidewalk to include the light standards, presumably designed by Bliss & Faville, and the boxed trees.

2. St. Francis Hotel

3. Saks Fifth Avenue
1981, Hellmuth, Obata & Kassabaum
364-85 Post St.

Qantas Building
1972, Skidmore Owings & Merrill
350 Post St.
Designed to be a background building between two ornate Classical neighbors, Qantas now looms blandly over the stripped palazzo that is Saks.

Bullock & Jones Store
1923, Reid Bros.
370 Post St.

Hyatt on Union Square
1972, Skidmore Owings & Merrill
345 Stockton St.
A well-mannered design with commercial space on the square and a mostly unshaded plaza. A special delight is the drought restricted fountain set into the plaza steps. Designed by Ruth Asawa, the bronze reliefs on the drum were cast from "bakers' clay," a flour, salt, and water dough modeled by family members, neighbors, and scores of school children into scenes of San Francisco.

4. Commercial building
1910, D. H. Burnham & Co., Willis Polk, designer
278-99 Post St.
A good example of a Neoclassical commercial building in which the "architecture" was designed to ride above the changing shop fronts.

Gump's
1861; rem. 1908, Clinton Day
246-68 Post St.
Originally built in 1861 but remodeled extensively after the fire, Gump's Gallery is the oldest continuously operating gallery in northern California. The department store actually evolved from the family's gallery and has continued to present the region's major trends in art and home furnishings.

5. Circle Gallery

5. Circle Gallery (former V. C. Morris Store)
1949, Frank Lloyd Wright; rest., 1983, Michele Marx
140 Maiden Lane
Although this design anticipated the Guggenheim Museum's celebrated spiral, it was actually a remodeling of an old building into a retail space for the Morrises, purveyors of fine crystal and other interior appointments. Greatly to their credit the gallery owners restored the neglected interior and reinstated Wright's furnishings.

6. Neiman-Marcus
1982, Johnson/Burgee
S.E. corner Stockton and Geary Sts.
Replacing a revered landmark, the 1896-1908 City of Paris store by Clinton Day and Bakewell & Brown, this design preserves the latter's great stained glass rotunda but not in its original central location.

6. Neiman-Marcus

7. I. Magnin & Co.
1946, Timothy Pflueger
233 Geary St.
This elegant skin, hung on a 1905 office building frame, was made flush to keep off the pigeons who, as Union Square's most numerous residents, should, after all, influence its architecture. The design was so successful with shoppers and so discouraging to pigeons that the same design was used in Seattle.

Macy's
1928, Lewis P. Hobart
101 Stockton St.
Rising above a marble-clad base, the conventionally composed pier-and-spandrel walls that retain their windows have the kind of eye appeal that is sadly lacking in the blank modern additions to the store on Union Square.

7. I. Magnin & Co.

8. Commercial building
1933
200-16 Powell St.
A Moderne jewel box that awaits restoration.

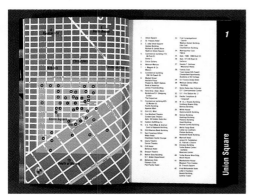

Typographic grids do not have to be complicated. They only have to be as complex as the information they organize. The spread shown above, for example is organized into two columns: a narrow one (9 picas) to place architectural photographs, and a wider one (17 picas) for the adjacent text that describes the photographs. Two picas separate the columns. Margins are 6 picas (top), 3.5 picas (outside), 3 picas (inside), and 4 picas (bottom). The size of the book is 6" x 9".

Only a few people v
sharply behind th
Hill was the prime
Andrew Hallidie in
1873 and then up Cali
perhaps because of its shape, but al
called "nabobs" (a word that once a
Big Four who controlled the all-pow

The book's division pages are accented with a bold drop cap consisting of a black circle and an italic, Helvetica Black Condensed letter reversed to appear as white. The text runs around the circle, with the capital *O* aligning with the text as indicated. Most page-layout applications enable you to easily run text around objects such as this circle and other images.

A well-designed publication is a community of types where all of the citizens work together for a common purpose: helping the reader navigate information. When community members stray from this goal, the result causes general mayhem on the page and undue violence to the reader. *Gifford Beal: Picture-Maker* is an exhibition catalog whose typographic elements work together to visually capture the spirit of the artist's paintings. Computer-manipulated type, uttering the forms, textures, and colors of Beal's paintings, serves also to express the thoughts of the catalog's author. A narrow carpet of space rolls through the catalog, linking all of the parts and providing a structure for a great many typographic expressions. Together, the type families Garamond and Futura make this expression possible.

On the cover, the name *BEAL,* set in Futura Extra Bold, is expressed as a bold pattern of letters and shapes. A technique used by the painter was to make black outlines of shapes and then fill them in with color. The outline letters reflect this process. Beal's lively canvases are revealed in the varied shapes of the letters, filled-in counters, shifted outline letters, and color. In this sense, typography functions as illustration. Notice the spatial corridor established by the height of the capital letters on the cover (far left). A yellow rectangle with a black letter *B* on the inside back cover provides a variation on this theme (left) and unity among the pages.

Gifford Beal: **Picture-Maker**

Every letter and every word consists of a unique pattern of shapes. An awareness of these shapes is important for an exploration of the many expressive possibilities inherent in typography. The key to our understanding is to perceive letters and words as an interaction of both positive and negative shapes. Letters consist of the familiar outer shell, but the shapes inside, between, and around them are an essential part of their anatomy. Several computer manipulations enabled the designer to create the typographic effects found on the cover. The outlined letters were created by generating letters on the screen, converting them to paths using a "convert to paths" command, and assigning a thin line to the outlined paths. The black shape defined by the space between the letters *E* and *A* was made by making a black rectangle, positioning it over the two letters, and "sending it to the back." The interplay of the shapes in the example below molds an expressive, highly visual word and picture.

When letters and their surrounding spaces touch or overlap and they are the same color, they share space. This visual effect is called "flooding." Flooding type leads to unusual spatial effects and is an excellent way to charge a page with suspense and visual ambiguity. The letter *A* above is flooded by the space between the letters. This principle can be applied to the design of headlines, logotypes, and and other special situations.

The horizontal band created by the letters on the cover is referenced on interior pages in a variety of ways. The spread below accomplishes this with the use of horizontal ruled lines on the verso page and a layer of Futura Bold text within a column of lighter Garamond text on the recto page. A detail of an actual column to the right illustrates how the darker tone of Futura Bold as well as its textural attributes distinguish it from Garamond.

attacked his canvas directly with the brush, rarely using any form of preparatory sketches. Spontaneity was achieved in the actual process of painting. Beal, on **the other hand, used on-the-spot sketches to familiarize himself with his subjects and to capture a sense of motion. These preparatory sketches, used to create his major paintings, were not only guides to the finished works but exercises, as he explained: "When one has known a subject for a long time, when one is familiar with all its aspects, when one has sought for what makes it beautiful, what gives it movement – then is the time to paint it, because most of the problems have already been solved in the painter's mind." Underscoring the importance of the close association between the active involvement of the mind while sketching and actually** composing the finished work, Beal stressed that these color sketches were "only useful to picture-making if used immediately. Memory fades out after some months," he explained, "and the eyesight work is all that is left." The next step in picture-making," as Beal put it, was to draw in your motif in regard to actual forms and spaces so that it obtains a sense of order."**13** Color, Beal maintained, is dependent upon form.

Typography often forms liaisons with other support elements to help make a point. For example, the captions for the paintings consist of type enclosed within L-shaped ruled lines. The lines terminate with small black dots that point to the paintings they are referencing (below left). In addition to the traditional arrow, many other pointing devices can be effectively used (below).

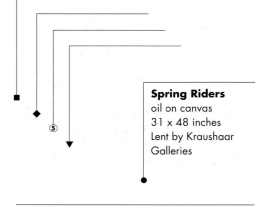

Spring Riders
oil on canvas
31 x 48 inches
Lent by Kraushaar
Galleries

A spread featuring paintings from the exhibition retains the same corridor structure as found on other pages, but in yet another variation. The letters B, E, A, and L define the corners of this space, providing a typographic signature for the paintings.

A date and descriptive text are located above the paintings. For emphasis, the date runs vertically on the page and is letter spaced for attention.

Designer:
Rob Carter

Typography has a wild, sometimes rebellious side, an expressive life beyond its assigned task as a system of symbols for sounds in human speech. People working with type must always make the decision of how tight to hold the typographic reins. If type is overly expressive it may drift from its original purpose – communicating an intended message. In the exhibition catalog, *A Golden Age of Painting,* the type is at once expressive and functional. Helvetica, the type family used in the catalog, is about as visually neutral as type can be, but its use can be highly expressive. Here, it explores the texture, color, tonality, and luminescence of sixteenth century Dutch landscape painting – not in a literal sense, but in an implied sense.

The first implication of a landscape appears on the cover. The first part of the title, *A Golden Age,* is half hidden, extending above a thin horizon line. The word *Golden,* printed in a yellow-gold color, corresponds to the word's meaning and suggests a rising sun. This phrase is repeated at a smaller size in three different weights of letter spaced Helvetica to create the illusion of depth and to signify a sprinkling of other possible terrain features. *Of Painting* appears further down on the page to complete the title.

A Golden Age

of

Painting

Dutch, Flemish, German Paintings
Sixteenth–Seventeenth Centuries
from the Collection of
The Sarah Campbell Blaffer Foundation
Houston, Texas

January 23–March 21, 1993

All of the page elements fit together in dynamic motion through detailed alignments and puzzle-like linking. And though not a typographic hair is out of place, the overall design is relaxed and fluid. An example of a caption carved out of the black shapes reveals the typographic variety achieved in this flexible system (right).

Figure 5

There are many ways to indicate paragraphs within text. One method is to insert a symbol between the last word of one paragraph and the first word of another. An ellipse is used to indicate paragraphs in this catalog (see spread below), and an endless supply of symbols are available for this purpose. Any dingbat or pictogram (a picture representing an idea) will do, but you are advised to consider the content of your message and choose one that relates. Many different symbol fonts are available for computer use, or you may design it yourself. A collection of the ubiquitous Zapf Dingbats offers a basic range of possibilities (below).

✕✖✗▢❑▢❒✳✴❁✼✻✽✹✺✶✷
❖■◆▲▼●○◍❂❁❍➀☎➠✉✁✎✄➡
✿✾✳✶✸✹✺✷☆✩✫✬✭✪✮✯✦✧✛✚✜
✢✱✲❀✻❥❦❣♡❦♣♤♠♦➢➢♠

Overlapping type, creating a sense of three-dimensionality and transparency, is a technique used on the pages of the catalog. Unfortunately, the indiscriminate layering and heaping of type upon type has in recent years become a visual scourge. Designers beguiled by the ease of computer operation and the tide of fashion fall into this trap. But when used sparingly and with just cause, layering promotes visual depth with the illusion of receding and advancing typographic elements. To ensure readability, there must be sufficient contrast in the color of the layered types (right).

Peter Paul

Rubens's greatest pupil, Anthony van Dyck, also created religious and myth example is his portrait of Antoine Triest, Bishop of Ghent **(fig. 6)**, which he e inspiration, but unlike Rubens, he had devoted his studies to the paintings o brushwork developed in a distinctively free and fluid manner, quite different the Southern Netherland not the least of which wa Calvin, Protestantism, h

The two spreads to the left provide a glimpse at the systematic arrangement of page elements. Pictures are vertically centered and pushed to the edge of the page. These anchor the space while other elements – black rectilinear shapes, artists' names in display type, text type, and captions – rotate around the pictures like planets around the sun. The artists' names are printed in colors pulled from the paintings, and the text blocks and captions vary in shape from page to page.

In a dazzling display of eccentric letter-forms, designer Larry Clarkson captures in this cover the contorted mystery of science fiction set in the Intermountain West. Computer distortions transform existing letters into unique and curious hybrid forms that tease a reader's imagination. These elements integrate with evocative photographs such as the Barrier Canyon pictograph with its haunting gaze. The controlled integration of contrasting letterforms provide the cover with compositional unity. Bernhard Tango, wispy and wind-blown, combines with a custom-stretched Futura to provide a most striking cover.

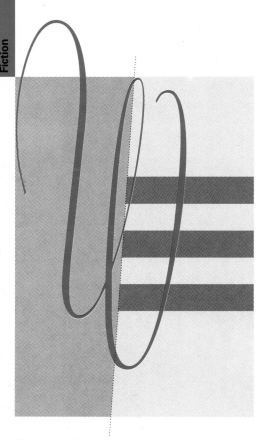

FUTURA 100%

FUTURA 120%

FUTURA 145%

FUTURA 165%

FUTURA 190%

FUTURA 215%

FUTURA 240%

The title of this book is set in Futura, horizontally scaled by the computer to 240%. The visual effect of such scaling is both a widening of the letters themselves and of their vertical strokes. Compare the top word set in normal (100%) Futura Regular to the horizontally-scaled versions. Notice how the widths of the letters change but the heights remain constant. If you have an urge to horizontally scale type, be forewarned that the result is an entirely different typeface with proportions unlike the original. Unless distorting typefaces in this manner appropriately supports the typographic message, discretion should be used.

IND

The cover is divided into two trapezoidal sections formed by a dominant diagonal line running from the top of the page to the bottom. These panels are divided further into smaller shapes housing photographs and typography. The large, serpentine Bernhard Tango *W* contradicts the severe geometry of the panels and softens the cover's appearance.

This detail from the book's spine shows how the integration of two totally unrelated typefaces can create an effective union. The flamboyant Bernhard Tango *W* serves as the initial cap for the word *Wind*.

Also, the meaning of the word *Wind* is reinforced by the letter *W*, which appears as if blowing in the wind. The computer enables the free exploration of such odd but effective type combinations.

These two letters belong to the same type family, Bernhard Tango, but the only similarity they hold is their name. The *W* on the top is the regular version; the one on the bottom is the swash version. Many type families possess such visual and stylistic variety. When selecting typefaces it is important to consider them on the basis of their visual characteristics, not on the basis of their name.

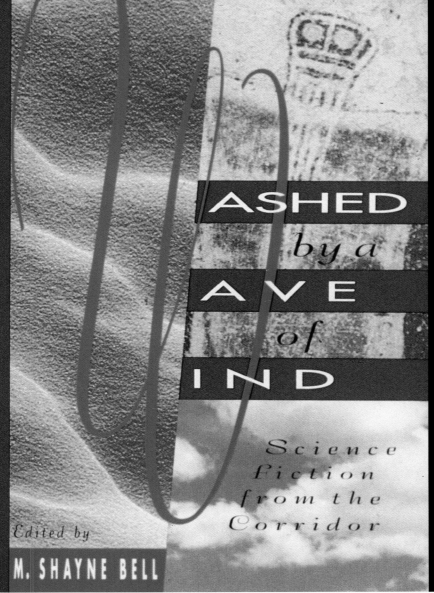

WASHED BY A WAVE OF WIND (spine)

BELL (spine)

Signature Books (spine)

WASHED
by a
WAVE
of
WIND

*Science
fiction
from the
Corridor*

Edited by

M. SHAYNE BELL

By scaling the letter *W* to a narrower width, and sizing and positioning it precisely, it functions simultaneously as the initial cap for the words *Washed, Wave,* and *Wind.* This large letter also binds together all of the elements of the cover into a unified whole. When you are faced with unifying several different elements on the page, assigning a dominant role to one of the elements is one method to accomplish this task.

Script typefaces can be extremely difficult to read when set in large amounts of text, but when used for emphasis and impact, as in the subtitle for this book cover, they can be very effective. Here, Bernhard Tango evokes a mood of mystery relating to the subject matter of the book. Notice also how the lines of type are aligned flush left on a diagonal. This effect is achieved by positioning each line, then fine-tuning their alignment using a kerning tool. Compare the optically adjusted example on the left to the unadjusted example on the right. The red arrows point to problem lines.

*Science
Fiction
from the
Corridor*

*Science
Fiction
from the
Corridor*

Designer:
David Colley

Consider the task of designing a 738-page book consisting entirely of text – a collection of scholarly papers. How does one devise a typographical system that at once promotes readability, establishes visual consistency and order among a large number of pages, and results in an inviting, visually harmonious design? *Marxism and the Interpretation of Culture,* published by the University of Illinois Press, is a book that emulates these attributes. Every detail of the design – from folios to footnotes – is painstakingly planned. The result is a book that transforms an otherwise laborious undertaking into a pleasant and serene reading experience.

edited and with an introduction by
Cary Nelson and Lawrence Grossberg
Marxism and the
Interpretation of Culture
Cornel West
Stuart Hall
Henri Lefebvre
Chantal Mouffe
Catharine A. MacKinnon
Paul Patton
A. Belden Fields
Étienne Balibar
Oskar Negt
Gajo Petrović
Ernesto Laclau
Christine Delphy
Gayatri Chakravorty Spivak
Perry Anderson
Franco Moretti
Fredric Jameson
Andrew Ross
Fred Pfeil
Eugene Holland
Julia Lesage
Michèle Mattelart
Fernando Reyes Matta
Simon Frith
Michael Ryan
Jack A. Amariglio
Stephen L. Resnick
Richard D. Wolff
Jean Franco
Stanley Aronowitz
Sue Golding
Richard Schacht
Armand Mattelart
Iain Chambers
Terry Eagleton
Michel Pêcheux
Hugo Achugar
Darko Suvin
Michèle Barrett
Fengzhen Wang

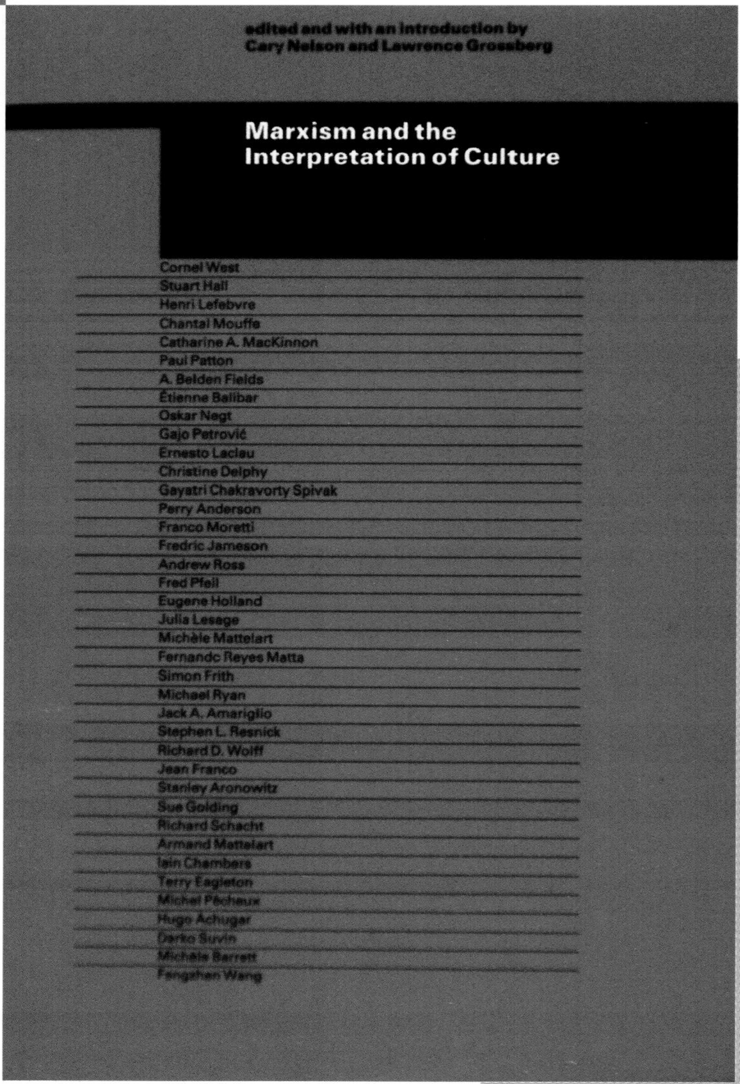

The book is designed to make the vast amount of information contained within it accessible to the reader, a goal accomplished by means of a well-conceived organizational structure and an effective typographic plan. Beyond these practical concerns, it is also a statement of simple beauty and formal precision. At a glance, the shockingly red cover presents the book's content, with a list of contributors nested within a wall of horizontally ruled lines. The title, appearing as white Univers 75 letters on a bold rectilinear shape, is the most prominent element on the cover.

In the venerable tradition of book design, there is a prescribed anatomy and sequence of parts. In order of appearance, the parts include front matter (blank leaves or end sheet, frontispiece, bastard title, title page, copyright page, dedication, foreword, preface, acknowledgments, contents, and illustration); text (sections, chapters, plates); and back matter (appendix, notes, bibliography, picture credits, glossary, index, colophon, blank leaves or end sheet). In contemporary book design, this traditional anatomy is flexibly interpreted, with new parts added, other parts deleted, and the order of the parts determined by the specific needs of the book.

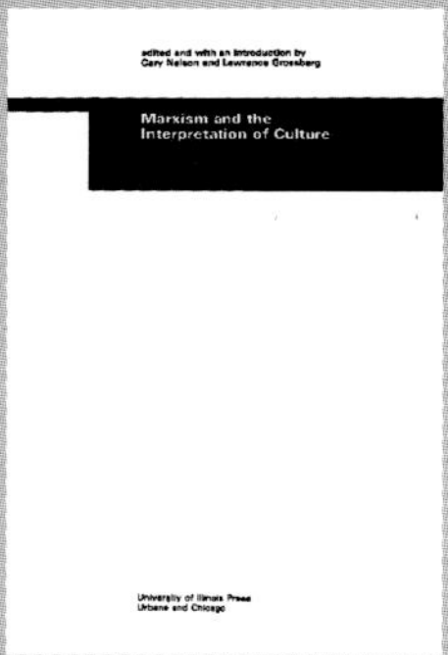

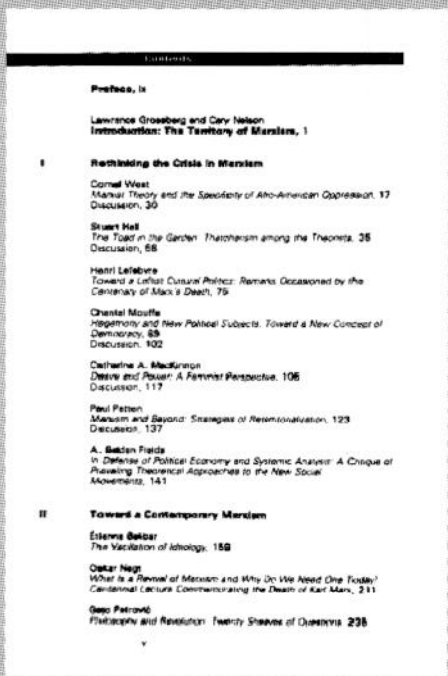

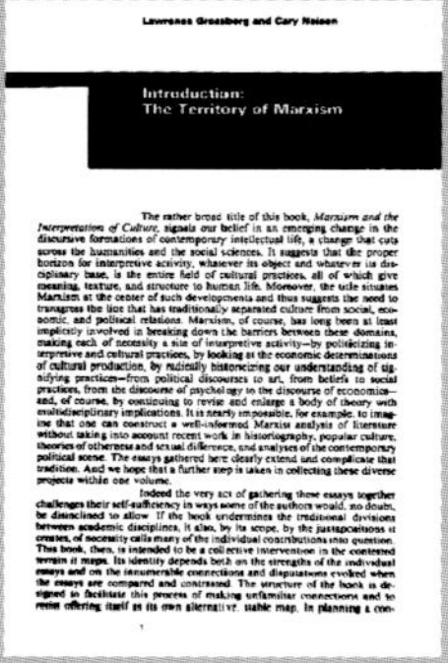

edited and with an introduction by
Cary Nelson and Lawrence Grossberg
Marxism and the
Interpretation of Culture

Preface, ix
Lawrence Grossberg and Cary Nelson
Introduction: The Territory of Marxism, 1
I Rethinking the Crisis in Marxism
II Toward a Contemporary Marxism

Lawrence Grossberg and Cary Nelson
Introduction:
The Territory of Marxism

Shown here in order of appearance are three representative pages from *Marxism and the Interpretation of Culture.* From top to bottom are title, contents, and introduction pages.

Whether simple or complex, every book manuscript possesses unique layout problems that must be specifically addressed by the designer. As you look at the two spreads to the right, you can see how David Colley resolved the integration of block quotations (left), and end notes (right).

The grid is the organizational scheme for the cover and interior pages. Here it is superimposed upon a page featuring an interview, so that you can see how the parts are adapted to it. Compare the use of the grid in this page with the others presented here.

Cornel West

Marxist Theory and the Specificity of Afro-American Oppression

As racial conflicts intensify in Europe, North and South America, Asia, and, above all, South Africa, the racial problematic will become more urgent on the Marxist agenda. A neo-Gramscian perspective on the complexity of racism is imperative if even the beginning of a "war of position" is to be mounted. In fact, the future of Marxism may well depend upon the depths of the anti-racist dimension of this theoretical and practical "war of position."

Will this statement be susceptible of understanding? In Europe, the black man is the symbol of Evil. . . . As long as one cannot understand this fact, one is doomed to talk in circles about the "black problem."
Frantz Fanon
Black Skin, White Masks

The problem of the twentieth century is the problem of the color-line—the relation of the darker to the lighter races of men in Asia and Africa, in America and the islands of the sea.
W. E. B. Du Bois
The Souls of Black Folk

As we approach the later years of the twentieth century, Fanon's characteristic candor and Du Bois's ominous prophecy continue to challenge the Marxist tradition. Although I intend neither to define their meaning nor defend their veracity, I do wish to highlight their implicit interrogation of Marxism. Fanon's and Du Bois's challenge constitutes the germ of what I shall call the *racial problematic:* the theoretical investigation into the materiality of racist discourses, the ideological production of African subjects, and the concrete effects of and counterhegemonic responses to the European (and specifically white) supremacist logics operative in modern Western civilization.[1]

I understand the issue of the specificity of Afro-American oppression as a particular version of the racial problematic within the context of the emergence, development, and decline of U.S. capitalist society and culture. This problematic is, in many ways, similar to contemporary philosophical discussions of "difference" that flow from the genealogical inquiries of Michel Foucault and the deconstructive analyses of Jacques Derrida.[2] Yet this problematic differs in that it presupposes a neo-Gramscian framework, one in which extradiscursive formations such as modes of production and overdetermined, antagonistic class relations are viewed as in-

17

Univers and Times Roman are the two typefaces used throughout the book. You will notice that these are presented in two different sizes only. A glimpse at the anatomy of an article opening reveals several other notable features.

The names of authors are set in 9 point Univers 75.

Dominating the page by virtue of size is the title set in 14/16 Univers 75. The scale of the title establishes hierarchical prominence, but it does not appear clunky on the page.

A brief introduction to the article – set in 8/10 Univers 55 – is reversed from a bold rectilinear shape to appear as white. Reversing type is another way of achieving emphasis, but is a technique normally reserved for smaller amounts of text.

A notable quote, also set in 8/10 Univers 55, appears on a short measure of 16 picas.

The main text introduces 10-point Times Roman, set with one point of lead on a 28-pica, justified measure.

New paragraphs are indicated with a first line indent of 8 picas. A strong vertical axis trails through the page, aligning the author, introduction, quote, indents, and folios for visual unity.

Designers:
David Colley
Jerry Hutchinson

This small book, precious to hold, was designed and printed as a promotional book to showcase exceptional two-color printing. Six colors and black appear as impeccable lithographed solids, and small black type printed on letterpress is crafted with deft refinement. Entitled *designer quotations,* the book presents quotes by fourteen well-known graphic designers and typographers. The name of each designer is typeset in a typeface that alludes to the designer's work and typographic sensibility. Designer quotations are set in Garamond. The computer was used to produce this book, but its presence is completely invisible. Refreshingly, the book reflects none of the trendy tricks often associated with the use of the computer; fine typography is its ultimate aim.

A trickling of open and closed quotation marks appearing as white on a black field emphasizes the book's content. When viewing the cover, one first comes upon the word *quotations,* as it is positioned at the left edge. The word *designer* hovers top and right. All of these elements appear in white, while the name of the printing firm, Dupli-Graphic, is printed in blue for emphasis.

Extending the cover's quotation mark theme, a single pair of open and closed quotation marks are grouped together in the center of the first and last pages. In contrast to the cover marks, these appear as black on white. This page serves as an introduction to the designer quotes, also centered on interior pages.

Background colors, typefaces, and type manipulations of designer names refer to attributes associated with the work and philosophical attitudes of the designers. For example, devices such as the use of black and white, bar rules, and reverses are intermittently found in Wolfgang Weingart's work. Stacking the two words also emphasizes the angular pattern of the letters *W,* and achieves a compact, rectangular shape. When devices such as this are used, type gains visual prominence, and ordinary words are transformed into pictures. Compare the name *Wolfgang Weingart* before and after the visual transformation (below).

Wolfgang Weingart

Wolfgang Weingart

"I am convinced that intensive investigation of elementary typographic exercises is a pre-requisite for the solution of complex typographic problems"

Massimo Vignelli

"Believe, express, and defend your responsibility towards society of not producing cultural trash."

The book is a statement of unencumbered simplicity, order, and refinement. The names of the designers appear consistently on the top half of each spread, while quotes are placed on the bottom half. Within this structured formula, variety is achieved through the specific positioning of designer's names, and a poetic arrangement of the quotes.

"Take risks based on what you have to gain rather that on what you have to lose."

"Believe, express, and defend your responsibility towards society of not producing cultural trash."

The quotes are broken down into logical thought units and arranged asymmetrically to amplify meaning. The two quotes reproduced here are attributed to the following designers: Rick Valicenti (top), Massimo Vignelli (bottom). Text aligned in the traditional flush left, ragged right manner – as in this paragraph – provides a very different reading experience.

The typefaces associated with each of the featured designers are identified below. Note the great diversity in their designs. When you are choosing typefaces for a particular project, try to select among the thousands available those that best suit the subject matter.

Designer	Typeface
Massimo Vignelli	Bodoni
Charles Eames	Helvetica
April Greiman	Universal Eight
Jan Tschichold	Sabon
Rick Valicenti	Oogabooga
Paul Rand	Stymie
Josef Muller-Brockmann	Helvetica Bold
Hermann Zapf	Palatino
Wolfgang Weingart	Akzidenz Grotesk
Eric Gill	Gill Sans
Frederic Goudy	Goudy
Laszlo Moholy-Nagy	Futura
Paul Watzlawick	American Typewriter
Robert Vogele	Spectrum

These representative pages show the range of typefaces and manipulations used to depict the designers. With minimal elaboration, the essence of each designer is revealed. Some depictions are achieved by simply showing well-known typefaces designed by the designers (Zapf and Tschichold); others require a combination of typefaces (Valicenti). Others, while still extremely elemental, require some elaboration (Greiman and Moholy-Nagy).

Rick Valicenti

April Greiman

Jan Tschichold

Hermann Zapf

LASZLO MOHOLY-NAGY

Designer:
Ned Drew

Two contrasting typefaces, Univers and Didot, artfully unite in the title of this book to represent the unprecedented transition to land privatization in Russia. Univers, simple and geometric, suggests the revolutionary art forms of El Lissitzky and Rodchenko at the time of the Russian revolution. Didot, mechanically severe yet as highly refined as polished silver, points to an era of democratization. One notices that where the letters "Rus" meet with the letters "sia" a transition occurs: an integration between two diverse letterforms and a symbolic evolution from the ideology of communism to the dream of democracy.

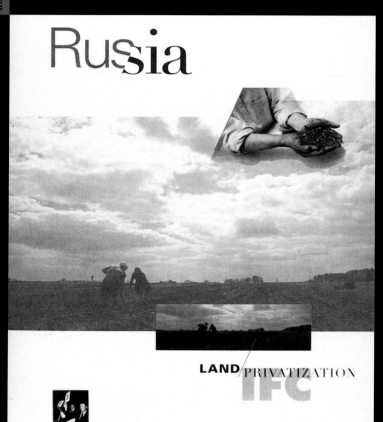

The cover of this booklet is organized by centering a large photograph of Russian farm workers. Bleeding from both edges, the photo establishes a stable space to which other elements are freely applied. A series of diagonal slashes represents the change from communism to land privatization, the first of which is created by splitting the word Russia in half. The first half of the word is set in Univers; the second half in Didot. The other slashes are lines printed in red ink. The privatization theme is further strengthened by the presence of three small, related photos. Together these elements unify the cover.

Using tone as a way of distinguishing and separating different parts of a typographic message can be very effective. The word *Russia* is composed of two shades of black, 50% and 80%. The more difference in the percentage of tone, the more difference in the separation of the typographic parts. Shades of black from 10% to 90% (left to right).

a a a a a a a a a a a

The booklet is published in two languages: English and Russian. The technique of joining two different typefaces into a single word seems to work better with the roman word *Russia* than with the Cyrillic word Россия, for the *s* letterforms establish a more evident diagonal line than do the Cyrillic с letterforms. But the joining of the с letters is not unsuccessful; the repetition of the two letters creates a visually interesting ligature.

Russia

Россия

heavy serifs | vertical stress | no bracket

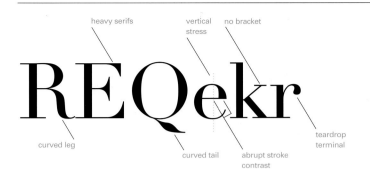

REQekr

curved leg

teardrop terminal

curved tail | abrupt stroke contrast

The Didot family of typefaces was the first to be categorized as "Modern." The original designs by Firmin Didot in 1784 predated by only a few years the ever-popular Bodoni family. The original Didot typefaces are more mechanically severe than Bodoni. For example, Didot serifs possess no brackets to soften the stroke-serif junction as does Bodoni. Didot's mechanical but elegant qualities make it a distinctive choice for book projects and applications requiring display type.

РОССИЯ

The Russian version of the booklet is identical to the English version, with the exception of the use of Cyrillic characters. The photograph of hands cupping soil calls out the idea of private land ownership in Russia, and the cropping of the image combined with the red rule line upholds the diagonal theme of the typography.

ЗЕМЕЛЬНАЯ/РЕФОРМА

Working with type requires a careful attention to detail at all stages in the design process. The diagonal split in the word *Russia* is accomplished by carefully aligning the two *S* letters, as indicated here. The red arrows reveal the points of contact between the letters. Adjustments such as this require an uncompromising attention to detail.

LAND/PRIVATIZATION

The subtitle typography corresponds to the title typography in that it also is composed of serif and sans serif typefaces, and the second part of the unit is positioned slightly lower than the first part. Repeating elements in this manner is one way of establishing visual unity within a typographic design.

Designers:
Barbara Glauber
Somi Kim

The way type looks – with its eccentricities, tensions, and visual noise – can tell a story beyond the meaning of the words; dirty, raw, and undisciplined type can express an attitude and reveal a personality. Whether considered beautiful or ugly, it communicates . . . something. In the case of The California Institute of the Arts admissions booklet, a wide selection of typefaces (all of which are designed by students, alumni and faculty of the school) combine with images and unusual color to express the exuberant personality of the school. Given their popularity, and the relative ease with which they are made, novelty typefaces will continue to surface and be used alongside the classics.

The designers of this booklet did a superb job of taking a carnival of outlandish and novelty typefaces and combining them into an expressive, and readable publication. In the hands of less astute designers, the use of these same typefaces could prove disastrous – the equivalent of a typographic train wreck. A recent trend in the use and misuse of rude and crude typefaces is referred to as "grunge" typography.

When choosing typefaces, consider those that are visually empathetic with the content you are representing. This is particularly true in the use of eccentric and decorative types. These are not appropriate for all purposes and occasions, for they may emit contradictory visual signals. Also, where there is a gain in visual effect, there is often a loss in readability. Using the experimental types designed by alumni and faculty of Cal Arts for this admissions booklet is quite effective in communicating the exploratory spirit of the school.

Printed in day-glo orange, blue, and metallic silver, the festive cover introduces in its title two outrageously individualistic typefaces: Jot, a script face designed by Jeffery Keedy, and an unruly, lasso-like outline face called Outwest, designed by Edward Fella. Circular diecuts reveal details of photos on the first page of the booklet (far left).

The tribe of typefaces used in the booklet are shown below. Determining how to use each of them in the publication presented the designers with a challenge (below).

ARBITRARY SANS
ONE IOTA
PLATELET
TRIBULATION
WORMWOOD

On the contents spread, dots containing page numbers cascade spontaneously downward, while circular photographs referring to the various schools within the institute dominate the space. Large numerals identify major divisions such as a portfolio of student work and information about each school. Here, several typefaces are featured, including Platelet, Wormwood, One Iota, and Outwest (left).

Letters in General
The hypothesis that there is an ideally correct form for each letter of the alphabet is just as erroneous as Geofroy Tory's simple assumption that there is a relation between the shapes

Letters in General
The hypothesis that there is an ideally correct form for each letter of the alphabet is just as erroneous as Geofroy Tory's simple assumption that there is a relation between

Letters in General

The hypothesis that there is an ideally correct form for each letter of the alphabet is just as erroneous as Geofroy Tory's simple assumption that there is a relation between the shapes

L E T T E R S   I N   G E N E R A L

The hypothesis that there is an ideally correct form for each letter of the alphabet is just as erroneous as Geofroy Tory's simple assumption that there is a relation between the shapes

Letters in General

The hypothesis that there is an ideally correct form for each letter of the alphabet is just as erroneous as Geofroy Tory's simple assumption that there is a relation between the shapes

Heads are introduced into this booklet in great variety, and in any publication, deciding how to treat them is a valid concern. Heads may be the same size and face as the running text, or a different size and face. Space may or may not separate them from the text. Variations in their use depends on the degree of emphasis and separation you wish to give them. The small sampling of heads to the left is meant only to suggest the vast number of possibilities available.

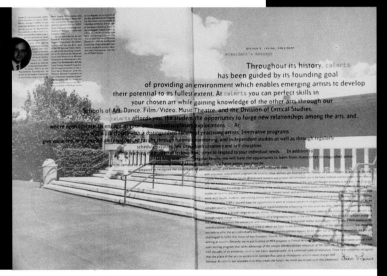

The size, placement, color, and use of white space determine the hierarchy of typographic elements, enabling the designer to guide the reader's eye around the page and through the information. On the three spreads shown here, type set asymmetrically in a typeface called Arbitrary Sans presents the text in a gradational progression, from large to small. The reader knows immediately where to begin, and is gradually immersed within the message.

Other distinctive devices used in the booklet are type printed on top of ghosted photographs for a layered look, and type that runs around circular photographs to create irregularly-shaped text blocks. As a whole, the publication is varied and complex.

On a spread listing alumni and their accomplishments, names set in Jot pop out in a hefty size. Accomplishments follow each name and are set in a long line of miniscule, squint-to-read Platelet. Perhaps justifying this text treatment is the fact that the information is not meant to be read from beginning to end as in the text of a novel, but informally browsed. This typographic usage creates a dazzling visual texture, a painterly canvas of type. Adding also to the textured effect is the use of thin, orange ruled lines rather than italics for titles, a touch that heightens the glow of the page.

The <u>hypothesis</u> that there is an ideally

The hypothesis that there is an ideally

When underlining type, it is best to avoid using the underline tool in computer application style menus. This method awkwardly severs the ascenders of lowercase letters (top). Avoid this problem by creating a separate ruled line and positioning it under the type (bottom).

In celebration of The Year of American Craft, KPMG Peat Marwick presented its entire craft collection to the Renwick Gallery of the National Museum of American Art, Smithsonian Institution. This book highlighting the exhibition reflects through its design, use of papers, printing, and choice of typefaces the inherent qualities of fine American crafts. Delicate type printed in subtle hues of green and brown appears understated on the page. Centaur, the book's text face, is set quite small due to mountains of information. Readability, however, is uncompromised, for Centaur maintains visual fidelity at reduced sizes, and the text has been carefully crafted with readability in mind. Two other typefaces add to the ambience of the book: Geometric 415 and Carpenter Script.

CONTENTS

In this detail of the contents page, we observe the compatibility of two very different typefaces: Centaur Regular and Geometric 415. The light and crisp Centaur with its refined serifs contrasts beautifully with the openness of the all capitals Geometric 415. Just as the distinct sounds of a guitar and piano in duet provide unique but blended qualities for the listener, contrasting letterforms provide uncommon voices capable of harmoniously separating different parts of information for the reader. Below, in a reproduction of the contents page, you can see how the abundant white space surrounding the type amplifies the fineness of the publication.

On the cover, the names of the artists whose work composes the collection are set in an elegant pattern of Carpenter Script. The script, suggesting well-crafted calligraphy, is printed in a brown ink just slightly darker in value than the earthy, textured paper. The catalog's centered title is set in 9.35 point Geometric 415, letter spaced for a distinctive look, and printed in light green ink.

Geometric 415

Carpenter Script

Centaur

Shown above are the three typefaces used in the catalog. Their compatibility lies not in their visual similarities, but in their differences. Geometric 415 serves primarily for use in heads, Centaur for the text, and Carpenter Script as the decorative pattern gracing the cover and endsheets. Finding just the right combination of typefaces for a given job requires a patient search.

BY THE SEA 1987

SISAL, LINEN, AND WOOL

47 X 96 X 5 IN.

(119.4 X 243.8 X 12.7 CM)

Generous letter spacing and leading in the lines of type composing the picture captions provide an airy texture and distinctly crafted appearance. Note the simplicity of this caption: one type size with the title distinguished from the rest of the information by using a bolder weight.

Scripts, which are typefaces based on calligraphy, are used primarily for display purposes. Some are quite simple while others possess flamboyant flourishes. In some scripts the connecting strokes of the letters touch one another; in others they do not. Compare the similarities and differences of Carpenter Script (top), Zapf Chancery (middle), and Zephyr Script (bottom).

script

script

script

DOMINIC DIMARE

In the mid-1960s Dominic DiMare, a San Francisco Bay Area junior high school art instructor and self-taught, part-time studio weaver, was in the vanguard of American fiber art. Using a multiple harness loom, quadruple weaves (four panels woven together at a single point), and warp manipulation, he fashioned sculptural hangings from a variety of yarns, threads, and natural fibers— horsehair, uncarded wool, even grasses.

Off the loom, the weavings were often twisted, rolled, pleated, and further shaped by interweaving wires, or by

A detail from an interior page, this well-crafted text column exhibits several excellent qualities and detailed adjustments.

The subhead is set in 7-point Geometric 415 Black, tracked to add 60/200-em space between the letters.

64-points of space separate the head from the text block.

The first line of the first paragraph is not indented. This is not necessary since no paragraph appears above it.

The main text is set on an easy-to-read 10-point measure with an average of 30 characters per line. The text is set in Centaur Regular, sized to 9.25 points with an ample 4.75 points inserted between lines. The alignment of the text is flush-left, ragged right.

The rag is rhythmic and visually consistent, with no distracting contours.

New paragraphs are indented with a 1-em space.

Compare the pattern composed of Carpenter Script reversed from a solid black background (below) to its appearance on the cover (facing page). You can achieve many different effects by simply changing the color of type and its background. Of course, something much more subtle was needed for this catalog, but color combinations with more exaggerated contrasts could work just fine in other situations.

The admissions booklet for the Southern California Institute of Architecture (*SCI-Arc*) defines the school as a "place of convergence and conflict, intersection and disjunction, where thoughts and sensibilities collide and conjoin." Typographically, the booklet emulates these principles with forms and textures conversing wildly in space. For the reader, each page turned reveals a new typographic experiment probing for new expressions and new definitions. Reading the booklet is not a quiet experience. It is not intended to be quiet; rather, its intention is to stir the imagination and confront the senses. The computer's role in the design of the booklet is evident in skewed, layered, and distorted type and images.

Reading and viewing the *SCI-Arc* booklet is an unpredictable experience. Photographs, lines, and type collide in a space teetering on chaos. The organization of these elements is asymmetrical, highly balanced, and controlled.

Many computer applications enable special effects such as the skewed type found on the *SCI-Arc* cover (opposite page). Unlike the effect achieved on the cover, however, these tools are frequently used to create effects that have little or nothing to do with communication content. The result is pure decoration, empty and meaningless, and equivalent to eating mounds of frosting without the cake. But such manipulations are legitimate when used intelligently to honor content. Legibility is also of concern when using these special tools, and even though type may be skewed, twisted, mirrored, layered, outlined, rotated, and curved, a degree of legibility and visual integrity can responsibly be preserved. The question is how far to go, and the answer lies in whether the effect enhances and supports the content and the readability of the message.

On the cover, the typographic acronym, *SCI-Arc*, emerges forward from deep within space. The skewed and warped letters, printed in a gradation of bright colors, appear on the page as a triangular flash of light. The letters are bitmapped, a reference to building and architecture, but their distortion suggests that *SCI-Arc* is a school committed to nontraditional, forward, and experimental teaching and thinking (right).

1

Southern California **Institute of Architecture**

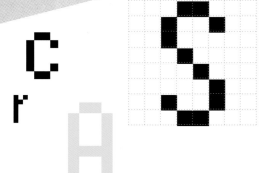

Bitmapped typefaces with their rectilinear, building block qualities are inherently architectural. Emperor, a bitmapped typeface based on a modular system of squares, is used in the booklet as both display and text type, but as text type it is used sparingly. Bitmapped typefaces do not possess the subtle design characteristics of more legible typefaces, but they are useful in specific situations. On the left is a collection of Emperor characters.

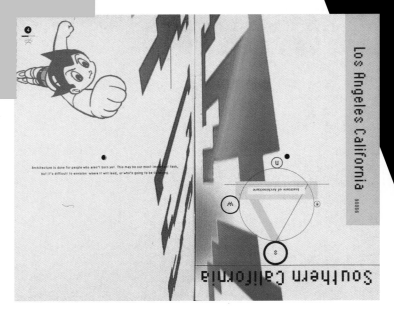

Los Angeles California 90066

Institute of Architecture

Southern California

Architecture is done for people who aren't born yet. This may be our most important task, but it's difficult to envision where it will lead, or who's going to be using it.

Re-emerging from time to time throughout the pages of the booklet, the *SCI-Arc* title assumes several warped variations. This recurring visual theme unifies the pages and periodically rein-troduces the drama of the cover. In the spread pictured here, a cartoon figure depicting a save-the-day superhero flies through a universe of visual form, a symbol of the goals and ambitions of the institute.

A small hole drilled through the center of the entire booklet adds a tactile dimension and reiterates a thought found on an interior page, "Architecture can punch a hole in your sky" (left).

A A A blend A

The blended color used on the title typography produces a striking visual image. Reversed from the black background, the color is greatly intensified. Using color blends for letters is an effective means to height-ened visual impact. If not used appropriately to aug-ment the content, however, the method is reduced to pure gimmickry. The most effective blends are those that use highly contrasting hues and values (left).

Text is treated differently from page to page, resulting in a panoply of textures and patterns.Type runs uphill, downhill, and upside down. The booklet's typography defies conventional legibility standards to convey to the audience the experimental nature of the school. On this spread, text with unusually wide word spacing creates a peppered texture that the reader must negotiate. This text is not easy to read; however, it is readable. Note how the yellow ruled lines keep the reader on course (right).

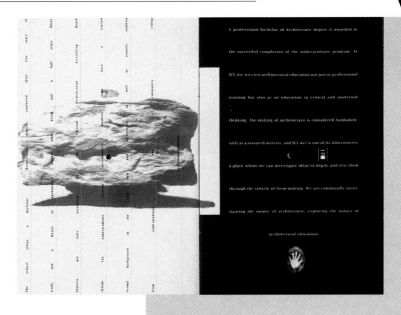

A professional Bachelor of Architecture degree is awarded at the successful completion of the undergraduate program. At SCI-Arc we view architectural education not just as professional training but also as an education in critical and analytical thinking. The making of architecture is considered fundamen-tally as a research activity, and SCI-Arc is one of its laboratories; a place where we can investigate ideas in depth, and test them through the vehicle of form-making. We are continually inves-tigating the nature of architecture, exploring the nature of architectural education.

Abstract and distorted images form odd, textured shapes that emerge, disappear, and re-emerge as the pages are turned (left).

Serving as a background for text, a black trapezoidal shape echoes similarly-shaped photographs. This relationship between different elements is called visual correspondence, the means by which diverse forms achieve unity (below).

Vertical lines of text reversed from bold, black rules are woven together with delicate, letter spaced lines. Both text blocks are abundantly line spaced and hover over a fading spray of paint (left).

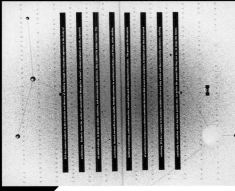

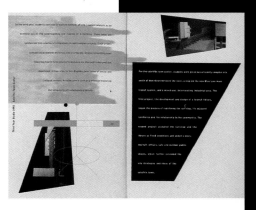

Examples of skewed text blocks and letters float buoyantly in space. The illusion of depth transforms normal pages into fascinating three-dimensional environ-ments. Despite their highly visual appearance, the text blocks maintain reasonable legibility. These techniques should be avoided when setting large amounts of text.

The hypothesis that there is an ideally correct form for each letter of the alphabet is just as erroneous as Geofroy Tory's simple assumption that there is a relation between the shapes of letters and the human body; erroneous, because the shapes of letters have been in consist[ent] process of modification from their very beginnings. Indeed, the shapes of letters now[?] daily use are due entirely to a convention, so th[at] in preferring one form to another our only consideration need be for the conventions now existing and the degree in which each satisfies our sense of beauty. It should be kept clearly in mind that "the perfect model of a letter is altogether imaginary and arbitrary. There is a definite model for the human fo[rm]. the sculptor, the architect, have th[e] nature. The the man who sets hims[elf] alphabet has no copy except that left [?] artists. . . . On all matters which pertain[?] fashion of his letter he has no absolute st[?]

On a page with a montage of computer-enhanced photographs and upside-down type, text reads: "Sci-Arc is an atmosphere in which faculty and students are encouraged not to fear failure but instead to fear not taking chances" (below).

The hypothesis that there is an ideally correct form for each letter of the alphabet is just as erroneous as Geofroy Tory's simple assumption that there is a relation between the shapes of letters and the human body; erroneous, because the shapes of letters have been in consistent process of modification from their very beginnings. Indeed, the shapes of letters now in daily use are due entirely to a convention, so that in preferring one form to another our only consideration need be for the conventions now existing and the degree in which each satisfies our sense of beauty. It should be kept clearly in mind that "the perfect model of a letter is altogether imaginary and arbitrary. There is a definite model for the human form. The painter, the sculptor, the architect, have their models in nature. The the man who sets himself to m[?] alphabet has no copy except which pe[?] artists. . . . On all matters which pe[?] fashion of his letter he has no [?]

Designer:
Kenneth J. Hiebert

Graphic Design Processes: Universal to Unique presents a philosophy of design based on the idea that simple, universal beginning points yield unique, varied, and novel design solutions. The design of the book is essentially a realization of its own premise. A modular grid is used throughout to organize the content, but its interpretation leads to dynamic transformations from chapter to chapter. Thumbing through the pages reveals rich and varied compositions and a sensitivity to rhythm and proportion. The computer is used as a tool to explore form, but not for the sake of form alone (this is decoration). Rather, it is used to understand the communicative potential of form, which includes the entire spectrum of words and images. The principal typefaces include Univers and Garamond 3 families, and DotLineCaps, a typeface designed by the book's author.

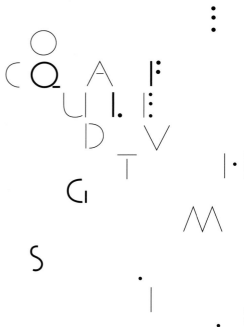

DotLineCaps, designed by Ken Hiebert and featured on the cover of the book, is a typeface of profound simplicity. It is composed entirely of dots and lines, the basic elements or building blocks of visual form. The typeface consists of two weights in two variations for nine of the letters. These letters awaken our primal consciousness; we have seen them before, throughout the millennia inscribed on steep rock walls, a reminder that we are not so far removed from our earliest ancestors. Compare DotLineCaps with the markings below. These petroglyphs are found in Nine-Mile Canyon, Utah.

The cover design reveals through type and supporting motifs the essence of the book's content. A stair-stepped line rule representing the design process ascends diagonally through the space to the subtitle, underscoring the word *Unique*.

Effective motifs such as this stepped rule are readily achieved with the computer. This is constructed with alternating horizontal and vertical rules.

The small red square combined with the word *Unique* calls attention to the word's meaning.

Unique

Kenneth J. Hiebert

Graphic Design Processes
...universal to **U**nique

"Creation

(discovery

during)

a

is

patient

search."

—**Le Corbusier**
(parentheses added)

Van Nostrand Reinhold
New York

This visually pleasing quote by Le Corbusier appears as an asymmetrical grouping of words on the title page (far left). Though the words stray from one another, the reader is able to decode the message by their relative positioning (they are still basically read from left to right, top to bottom as in standard reading). Visually, the quote implies the process of creation. The words *(discovery during)* are exaggerated by appearing as white letters on bold black bars. The total configuration is unified by the L-shaped border. Poetic type configurations such as this are not unlike painting with words.

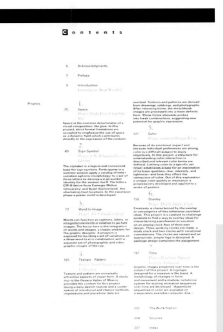

Contents

2.

49   **Sign-Symbol**
Project: CM–B Summer Session Identity

The alphabet is a logical and convenient base for sign-symbols. Participants in a summer session apply a catalog of letter variation options (morphology) to a set of three letters to develop a sign-symbol identity for the session itself. The letters CM–B derive from Carnegie Mellon (University) and Basel (Switzerland), the alternating host locations. In the expansion phase a poster motif is developed.

A detail from the contents page (far left) effectively utilizes different variants of Univers and Garamond 3 families. The prominent numeral *2* identifies the chapter; the folio appears sandwiched between two horizontal rules for easy identification; and the "project" line is set in italics for separation from the chapter title and blurb. The axis formed by the alignment of these elements and their positions (see dotted line) provides the orderly appearance of a well-pruned tree.

Design history is to creative new beginnings what memory is to experience: glossed, reduced, optimized, idealized.

In a world of appropriation, imitation, revivals, forgeries, of copious information exchange, of quotation of quotation of quotations, of myriad results seen out of context, the key question in learning is: where do we start?

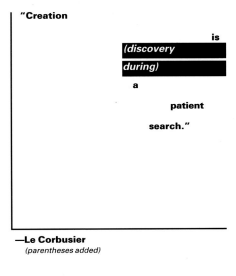

A representative detail from a text variation in the book reveals a very readable column of 10/12 Garamond 3 set to a measure of 21 picas. Of interest is the method for identifying new paragraphs, which is to use a 1-pica hanging indent for the first line of each paragraph. This clearly distinguishes one paragraph from another.

Geometric shapes are used on a division page to boldly divide the space, and to create a playful environment for the type.

"Play is a symbolic activity . . . its rules may be broken, or new rules invented, without leading to serious consequences. In play it is possible to go to extremes, to be daring, to experiment, so that the boundaries of the permissible and the practical can be tested to the full."
—James Gummo

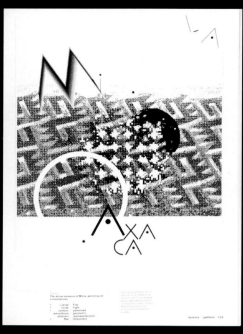

The three examples appearing on this page are experiments related to typographic texture and pattern. Each experiment explores variations of six basic aspects of texture: unit size, proximity, arrangement, unit shape, content, and physicality. These are broken down further into the contrasts listed in the morphological chart (chart of visual possibilities) shown below. Bold, horizontal ruled lines adequately separate each unit of information within the chart, and the centered lines of type with the aligned colons provide a clear and easy-to-follow structure. The specific aspects addressed in each experiment are marked with a bullet. The many textural qualities achieved in the experiments involve spontaneous computer manipulations such as repeating, overlapping, and layering.

Theme:
The stone mosaics of Mitla, astrological connotations

•	coarse :	fine
•	loose :	tight
•	random :	patterned
	amorphous :	geometric
	abstract :	representational
•	flat :	illusionary

Each experiment is based on a theme derived from a trip to Oaxaca Valley, Mexico. Texture transforms a physical site into a celestial environment related to the dependence on the movements of stars of early Mesoamericans. The floating *M* expresses a kinetic, three-dimensional heavenly body (above).

A dark and diffuse texture reveals the shadowy mystery of the stone mosaics of Mitla. The overlapping letters composing the logotype *Mexico* suggest a stone relief (left).

Patterns of varying texture and tone intersect to provide visual points of interest, particularly where the letters and abstract patterns overlap (above).

Poster 2:
A progression toward
lightness, brightness, and
linearity.

universal

unique

Simple, abstract shapes are typographic support elements that provide dynamic spatial environments for letterforms. The examples shown to the left and below are pages from a chapter on color and feature typographic compositions combining letterforms with squares, rectangles, circles, lines, and amorphous shapes of various colors. The computer is used as a visual "processing" tool or palette to spontaneously generate, organize, and integrate typographic forms and to assign effective, contrasting color. Upon comparing the compositions, you will notice that each is founded on the same base structure. Subtle shifts of planes and words, and energetic shifts in color demonstrate the potential for endless visual possibilities.

On each of the pages, a running foot composed of the title of a chapter and a visual symbol codifying the contents of the chapter are grouped with the folio. This verbal/visual method of mapping the pages makes it easy for the reader to determine where he is. An example of a running foot can be seen in the lower right corner of the above example. Identifying a chapter on color, the running foot's zig-zag motif relates to the poles of contrast in color: warm/cool, bright/muted, light/dark.

Designer:
Mirko Ilić

Two of the great icons of American pop culture, Elvis Presley and Marilyn Monroe, live on, immortalized in the adoring eyes of the American public. The book, *Elvis + Marilyn: 2 x Immortal,* contains a record of the Elvis-Marilyn myth, articles and famous images that preserve the King and glorify the Sex Goddess. Elvis and Marilyn are also immortalized in the book's design and typography. Bigger-than-life letters composing the title of the book and forming article texts fill entire spreads, enshrining the memory of Elvis and Marilyn. Here, typography provides not only a record of thoughts and events; it also heightens and perpetuates a popular myth.

The contents spread (top right) and a sample interior spread (bottom right) show the integration of type and image. Artists' statements at the tops of pages consist of centered lines of type that begin wide and progress to a point. This symmetry corresponds to the cover.

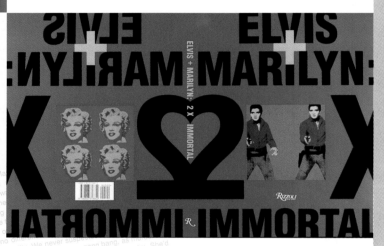

Images of Elvis on the front cover and of Marilyn on the back cover are framed within a mirror-image composition. Helvetica Black Condensed letters provide this symmetrically organized cover with dramatic presence. The facing numerals form a heart shape, a symbol of America's undying love for Elvis and Marilyn (above).

ELVIS MARILYN

Several spreads show variations in the text-formed title letters that run throughout the interior of the book (opposite page). These letters are constructed by running text blocks around shapes created with drawing tools. Essentially, the shapes define and "carve out" the counterforms of the letters. A runaround tool is used to specify the intervals of space between the shapes and the text. The diagram below indicates the shapes (described in yellow) defining the letter *R*.

A carefully aligned + sign, which is the same thickness as the vertical stroke of the letter *I* in *MARILYN* and the space between the two names, provides the title with visual unity and reminds us of the similarities between the two legendary celebrities.

ELVIS + MARILYN: 2 X IMMORTAL

Wendy McDaris

MARILYN, WE HARDLY KNEW YOU

Kate Millett

ELVIS PRESLEY: CHARACTER AND CHARISMA

Bruce Heller and Alan C. Elms

ELVIS, GLADYS, AND VERNON

The most absorbing books are often those that depart from conventional publishing practices – limited-edition books that are experimental and self-published. This book, which is the documentation of a graduate thesis project, is the author's search for meaning in the seemingly chaotic world of words and images. Whereas most books are designed to lead readers sequentially through the pages, this one can be read from front to back or from back to front. Either direction offers a valid journey, and the reader is encouraged to freely process and interpret the content. The book's typography ventures boldly into expressive realms without a significant loss in clarity and readability.

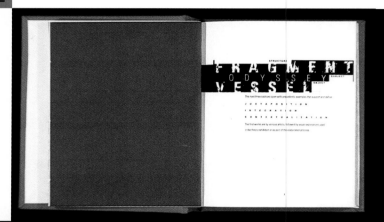

The tremendous variety achieved in the pages is not the result of using many different typefaces, but of combining type and images in a myriad of ways. In fact, the type, which excludes everything but the Univers family, is characterized by the use of small sizes and letter spaced capitals for heads. The text is set in condensed Univers 57 and 67 to conserve space and provide a distinct vertical texture.

A collection of spreads reflect a panorama of typographical experiments. Words and images are combined to offer a multitude of visual experiences and interpretations for the reader. When words and images are combined, their union unequivocally affects a reader's perception of the message. On a page shown on the upper right, for example, a scientifically-drawn image of a human heart is juxtaposed with a list of verbal cues to imply various emotional states.

integration
The sirens represent an
example of integration
because they were the
synthesis of half bird and
half woman.

BIRD / SIREN / WOMAN

And they entrance victims. Whoever
unaware comes close and hears the
siren's yodel will nevermore draw near
family, home, or infants, never share
such joys again.

They had b e a u t i f u l voices
and lured men to death and
d e s t r u c t i o n by their every
h a l f grotesque b o d i e d
h a l f

Knead sweet wax and
stop your shipmates' ears so
none of them will hear the
sirens sing. But if you wish to
listen to their song, have
your men lash you to the
mast, you can delight in
the sweet chant.'

16

The book contains numerous
typographic illustrations that
combine words and images
into dynamic compositions.
Shown here, in selections
from *The Odyssey* of Homer,

images of wings, and the
human figure whirl about one
another in space. Type placed
at angles appears in flight,
with airy line spacing
providing a feathery effect.

Two sample pages reveal the
emphasis placed on simple,
readable text, as well as on
the desire to strike an expressive chord. The text, appearing as 8/11, Univers 57, is
accentuated with elements
called out in the heavier
Univers 65. The word

SYNTHESIS begins on one
page with the letters *SYN*
(left), and is completed on the
next page with the letters
THESIS (right). On these
pages, the text runs vertically
rather than horizontally.

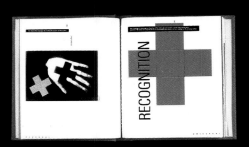

RECOGNITION

Ruled lines frame the table of
contents, providing a
structure that establishes a
clear hierarchy. The hierarchy
is further pronounced with
main titles set in letter
spaced, all-capitals Univers
67; and secondary titles set in
lower case, Univers 57 letters.
Positioning *TABLE OF
CONTENTS* to the left of the

adjacent information gives it
prominence on the page. Any
successful organization of
typography requires an
understanding of those parts
of the information that need
emphasis over others. In
other words, one must study
and understand the inner
logic of the text.

TABLE OF CONTENTS

research
documentation

Ruled lines are typographic
support elements that aid the
designer in organizing type
on the page. Choosing just
the right ruled line or
combination of lines is no
arbitrary task. A heavy, solid
ruled line, for example, is

more assertive than a
delicate, dotted ruled line.
Some lines are simple and
functional; others are
elaborate and ornamental.
Below are a few examples
taken from a vast collection
of possibilities.

Designers:
Brian Lane
Henry Vizcarra

En Route features a collection of airline labels from the dawn of air travel to the beginning of the jet age. These colorful labels convey an evolution of decorative design styles – Art Deco and Pictorial Modernism being the most evident of these. The book's design suggests the flavor of these styles, and it stirs in the reader a nostalgia for the time when air travel was considered to be risky business, adventurous, and exciting. Period black and white photographs of smiling passengers and shiny aircraft complement streamlined typefaces and a friendly script. This eclectic design approach, which is guided by an appreciation of the past, is sometimes referred to as *Retro*.

The streamlined title letters on the cover are remniscent of the popular Art Deco Style of decoration and architecture during the 1920s and 1930s. The style is characterized by the use of geometrical and rectilinear shapes. The aircraft designs and labels of this period exhibit similar visual tendencies. The cover typography is symmetrically organized, just as it is on the label featured on the cover. Upon seeing the cover, the eye immediately focuses on the title, *EN ROUTE*. Color, size, and position on the page render it the most dominant of the elements. Note the top-to-bottom hierarchy of the type: the title appears as the largest element, the subtitle as the second largest, and the author line as the smallest (left).

EN ROUTE

LABEL ART FROM THE GOLDEN AGE OF AIR TRAVEL

BY
LYNN JOHNSON & MICHAEL O'LEARY

An airplane zooms across the contents spread with the reader on board for a tour of the world of airline labels. The dynamic motion of the plane is duplicated in the shape of the contents typography; it too is in flight, encouraging the reader to turn the page. The letter spaced Futura letters naming the chapters suggest movement, mimicking the red ruled line extending horizontally from the image of the airplane (right).

Holly Script

Script typefaces add an informality to publications. They work well in display settings such as headlines. Avoid using them for lengthy texts; other typefaces are more suitable for this purpose. Holly Script is the script typeface used in this publication (above right).

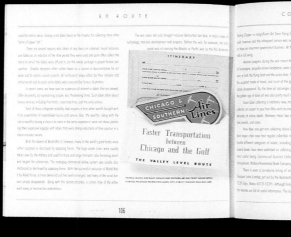

A nostalgic photograph faces the opening page of a chapter, and the chapter title, typeset in Holly Script, lends a friendly, handwritten appearance. These elements stand in contrast to two columns of mechanical Futura Condensed text type, set 10.5/18. The rigidity of the text is softened as it runs around an airline label turned at an angle on the page. The interplay of contrasting formal and informal elements adds a sparkling quality to the book (left).

Two ruled lines printed in grey stretch across the top and bottom margins of each page, creating a zone for the collection of labels and the main text. Above and below these ruled lines are the headlines, running heads, and folios (left). When using ruled lines to divide and frame the space of the page or to emphasize elements, it is recommended that you limit the number of different weights to as few as absolutely needed. Too many lines in too many weights will transform the page into a three-ring circus. Of course, there will be exceptions to the rule as appropriateness dictates. One other thought: when using multiple ruled lines on a page, an obvious contrast in weight is desirable. For example, it is better to make two lines of almost identical weight the same weight to avoid ambiguity. Presented below is a selection of ruled lines in different, contrasting variations and weights.

.25 pt

.35 pt

.50 pt

.75 pt

1 pt

2 pt

4 pt

6 pt

8 pt

10 pt

A versatile type family will always offer a wide range of weights. This is true of Futura, the fitting geometric typeface for this publication. Below are the representative weights, from underfed Light to overfed Extra Bold (below).

futura light
futura book
futura regular
futura bold
futura heavy
futura extra bold

Tiny and timid type set in Futura Book identifies chapters at the foot of each page. Sandwiched between these elements are larger folios set in Modula. The delicate effect of the letters is as much a result of the extreme letter spacing as it is of their size (above). Letter spacing, which is a function of tracking, entirely changes the visual texture of type. Used with discretion, it can emphasize or de-emphasize type elements and bring visual resonance to the page.

Designer:
John Malinoski

This museum catalog features the work of folk artist Ned Cartledge. Cartledge's relief paintings are colorful, naive, mischievous, and raw. The design of the catalog reflects these qualities and emphasizes through typography Cartledge's political nature and his need to express man's inhumanity to man. Frutiger functions as the primary typeface; its quirky and primitive qualities make it an excellent choice for the text. It is also a highly readable typeface, but less formal and rigid than other sans serif typefaces such as Univers or Helvetica. Typography has the ability to articulate and extend ideas within the content by virtue of its visual form. The display typography featured on selected pages of this catalog indeed reinforces ideas commonly found in the work of Ned Cartledge.

Ned Cartledge

Anderson Gallery
School of the Arts
Virginia Commonwealth
University

cloak of justice

under the cloak of justice

Consistent with the highly provocative nature of the catalog's content, the title of the publication begins on the back cover. Not immediately apparent to the reader, this device provides a double reading. Folded, the cover title reads *cloak of justice*. When the book is unfolded to reveal both the front and back covers, the entire title, *under the cloak of justice,* emerges. Curiously, the word *under* appears on the underside, or the back cover of the catalog.

I'm not inspired, I'm provoked.

With the computer, you can readily test many different type sizes and configurations. A detail from the opening page reveals a quote by the artist – an agitated and resonant quote. The large scale, bold setting and calculated line breaks contribute to its overall effectiveness. Visual unity occurs with the alignment and repetition of the two capital *I* letters; visual contrast occurs with the lower-case *i* nested between them.

Under the Cloak of Justice
the work of Ned Cartledge
Introduction by Robert Hobbs
essay by Joan Muller

An exhibition
organized
by the
Anderson Gallery
School of the Arts
Virginia
Commonwealth
University

Because it is the x-height and not the point size that determines the actual size of type, you should always base type size selections on visual appearance. Also, typefaces with larger x-heights, such as Frutiger, are generally considered more legible than typefaces of the same size with smaller x-heights. Compare the x-heights of 36-point Frutiger Roman, News Gothic, and Bodoni Book.

Frutiger
News Gothic
Bodoni

A rule selected and dragged over the title page typography is positioned with extreme accuracy. Aligned with the cross strokes of the lower-case *e*, it cancels out the notion of justice.

The catalog text is set in 8/10 Frutiger Roman, flush-left, ragged-right on an 11-pica measure (left). This text alignment creates very consistent word spacing, a quality that enhances readability. Compare this to the justified setting at the same type size and measure. Due to the inconsistent word spacing resulting from the justification, the text block appears scraggly and hard to read. Although commonly used, justified text is more difficult to read than flush-left, ragged-right text due to inherent word spacing problems. If you wish to set justified text, try using a longer line length than the one used here. This will greatly reduce the spacing difficulties.

I'm not inspired, I'm provoked.

Ned Cartledge

While Cartledge's sharp commentaries on the human condition are often tempered by his puns and double meanings, the artist's genial and soft-spoken personality still surprises. Born October 1, 1916, in the small north Georgia farming community of Canon, Cartledge had been whittling and carving since boyhood. While serving in World War II, he witnessed the results of the Holocaust in Germany. After the war Cartledge returned to Atlanta where he had a long career in the cotton industry, followed by a shorter one selling tools for Sears, Roebuck. His respect for tools and wood is evident in the careful craftsmanship of his carvings.

While Cartledge's sharp commentaries on the human condition are often tempered by his puns and double meanings, the artist's genial and soft-spoken personality still surprises. Born October 1, 1916, in the small north Georgia farming community of Canon, Cartledge had been whittling and carving since boyhood. While serving in World War II, he witnessed the results of the Holocaust in Germany. After the war Cartledge returned to Atlanta where he had a long career in the cotton industry, followed by a shorter one selling tools for Sears, Roebuck. His respect for tools and wood is evident in the careful craftsmanship of his carvings.

Designers:
John Malinoski
Matt Woolman

While traditional books provide cozy retreats upon entrance into their pages, this museum catalog, entitled *repicturing abstraction,* challenges established typographic conventions, alerting readers to a heightened awareness of typographic detail. Metaphorically, the catalog's typography "repictures" or "redefines" the idea of the book, but not at the expense of legibility. For example, the ISBN number, normally underplayed, appears as the largest element on the back cover; the catalog's spine spills onto the front cover, assuming a dominant visual role; and the title type on the cover fragments into smaller letterform parts. The Univers family of typefaces offers a versatile selection of typeface weights and widths for this rebellious, conceptual approach.

Typographic forms such as the oversized ISBN number, fragmented letters, and rectangular shapes dissolve the boundaries of the front cover, back cover, and spine. While visually supporting the "abstraction" theme, this shared space also provides cohesiveness.

In a detail of the spine, letters composing the word *abstraction* mirror the word's meaning by straying in all directions from their baseline.

Words of the title, repicturing "abstraction," align perfectly to form a unified rectangular shape as indicated by the blue box. As if falling apart, these words disassemble into fragmented letterform parts. This is achieved with the computer by selecting letters, separating them into parts, and then positioning the abstracted parts as needed.

In order to preserve the integrity and identity of the letterforms, the letters on the front cover are separated into parts at logical junctions. For example, the small red squares on the letter *a* indicate where this letter is divided (below).

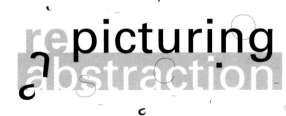

introduction

At every opportunity in the catalog, the four designated colors – orange, blue, red, and green – are introduced in various type elements as a means of referring to the participating museums. This system also provides color-coding to identify different sections of the catalog.

Applying these colors to the word, "introduction," produces a typographic rainbow and a distinctive visual sign.

The introduction spread utilizes color bars to call-out from the text the specific exhibitions occurring at each of four participating galleries.

An angled line leads the eye from the introduction text to a list of museum directors, also set at an oblique angle.

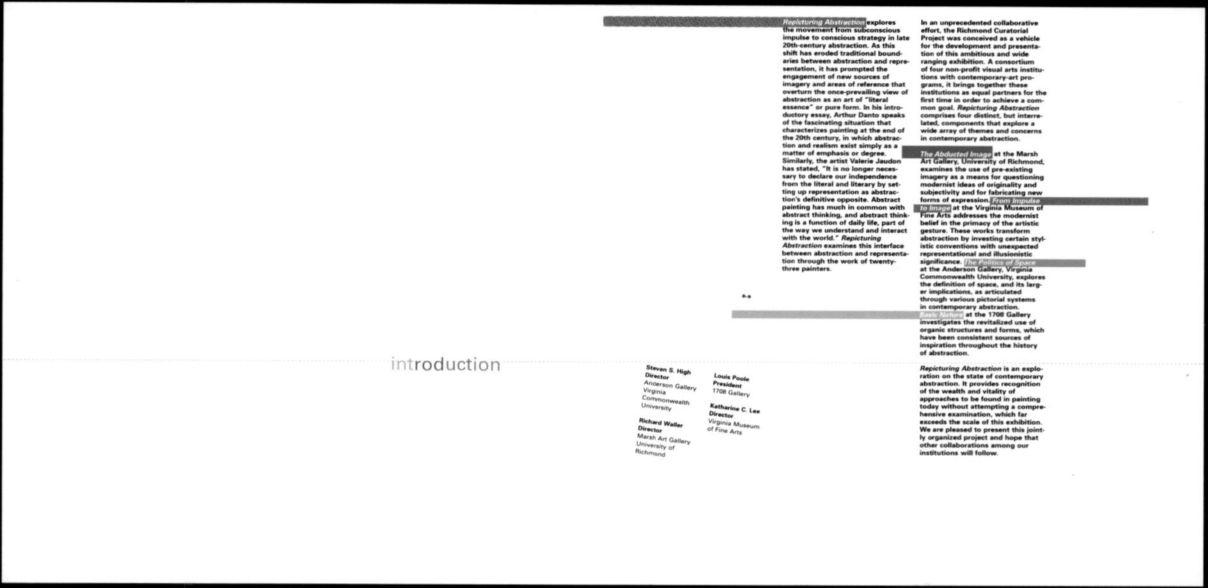

Repicturing Abstraction explores the movement from subconscious impulse to conscious strategy in late 20th-century abstraction. As this shift has eroded traditional boundaries between abstraction and representation, it has prompted the engagement of new sources of imagery and areas of reference that overturn the once-prevailing view of abstraction as an art of "literal essence" or pure form. In his introductory essay, Arthur Danto speaks of the fascinating situation that characterizes painting at the end of the 20th century, in which abstraction and realism exist simply as a matter of emphasis or degree. Similarly, the artist Valerie Jaudon has stated, "It is no longer necessary to declare our independence from the literal and literary by setting up representation as abstraction's definitive opposite. Abstract painting has much in common with abstract thinking, and abstract thinking is a function of daily life, part of the way we understand and interact with the world." *Repicturing Abstraction* examines this interface between abstraction and representation through the work of twenty-three painters.

In an unprecedented collaborative effort, the Richmond Curatorial Project was conceived as a vehicle for the development and presentation of this ambitious and wide-ranging exhibition. A consortium of four non-profit visual arts institutions with contemporary-art programs, it brings together these institutions as equal partners for the first time in order to achieve a common goal. *Repicturing Abstraction* comprises four distinct, but interrelated, components that explore a wide array of themes and concerns in contemporary abstraction.

The Abstracted Image at the Marsh Art Gallery, University of Richmond, examines the use of pre-existing imagery as a means for questioning modernist ideas of originality and subjectivity and for fabricating new forms of expression. *From Impulse to Image* at the Virginia Museum of Fine Arts addresses the modernist belief in the primacy of the artistic gesture. These works transform abstraction by investing certain stylistic conventions with unexpected representational and illusionistic significance. *The Politics of Space* at the Anderson Gallery, Virginia Commonwealth University, explores the definition of space, and its larger implications, as articulated through various pictorial systems in contemporary abstraction. *Erotic Nature* at the 1708 Gallery investigates the revitalized use of organic structures and forms, which have been consistent sources of inspiration throughout the history of abstraction.

Repicturing Abstraction is an exploration on the state of contemporary abstraction. It provides recognition of the wealth and vitality of approaches to be found in painting today without attempting a comprehensive examination, which far exceeds the scale of this exhibition. We are pleased to present this jointly organized project and hope that other collaborations among our institutions will follow.

introduction

Steven S. High
Director
Anderson Gallery
Virginia
Commonwealth
University

Richard Waller
Director
Marsh Art Gallery
University of
Richmond

Louis Poole
President
1708 Gallery

Katharine C. Lee
Director
Virginia Museum
of Fine Arts

There is an inexhaustible number of ways of creating openings for text. A method used for this catalog is to set the first word of the paragraph as a separate unit, rotate it, and position it in proximity to the paragraph at an askew angle (right).

The specifications of the text shown below promote readability. The typeface is Univers 55 set 8/10 with normal letter spacing. The line spacing separates the lines into distinguishable units, and the 13-pica column width allows enough characters per line for fluid reading.

Notes appearing at the ends of articles resound with kinetic vibrance. Horizontal ruled lines and rectilinear text are contradicted by diagonal ruled lines and numerals aligned at different angles.

Notes

1   James Meyer, "Mel Bochner: the Gallery is a Theater," *Flash Art* (Summer 1994): 142.
2   Meyer, 101.
3   Mel Bochner, "Out of Context. Mel Bochner," *Tema Celeste* (July-September 1989): 63.
4   Per Kirkeby, as quoted in Michael Peppiatt, "Good Painting is more kitschy than tasteful," *Art International* (Spring/Summer 1991): 45.
5   Gregory Galligan, "Per Kirkeby, the Ludwig Museum Retrospective," *Arts Magazine* (October 1987): 87.
6   Dana Friis-Hansen, "Painting Aether," *Rebecca Purdum* (Cambridge, Mass.: MIT List Visual Arts Center, 1991), 3.
7   Friis-Hansen, 7.
8   Hubert Damisch, *The Origin of Perspective* (Cambridge, Mass.: The MIT Press, 1994), 40.
9   Yves Alain Bois, *Painting as Model*, (Cambridge, Mass.: The MIT Press, 1990), 162.
10 Bois, 247.
11 Robert Steiner, *Toward a grammar of abstraction: modernity, Wittgenstein and the painting of Jackson Pollock* (University Park: The Pennsylvania State University Press, 1992), 15.

36-37

In

the early 1980s there appeared to many in the New York artworld to be a return to greatness after a decade of diffuse and inconclusive experimentation. It consisted primarily in a return to painting, and above all to an heroic kind of painting, vast in scale and ambitious in pictorial intention. The critic Thomas McEvilly enshrines this event in the title of his 1993 book, *Exile's Return*, which qualifies his epic characterization in his subtitle:

table of contents

Furthering the theme of the exhibition, liberties are taken with the contents page that push the typography to the edge of abstraction. A network of rule lines cross one another like a highway system, linking the contents of the catalog to corresponding page numbers.

Deciphering the information is challenging for the reader, but not impossible. Visual and expressive typography often requires a higher level of reader/viewer participation than do more conventional approaches (above).

A cluster of typographic elements appearing to float in space is sometimes referred to as a visual constellation. Such a grouping of elements is not random, and though indeed they appear vigorously kinetic, their positioning is deliberate. Typography functioning as a credit for artwork pictured in the catalog spins around a central letter *w*, a mirrored enlargement of the same letter found in the name of the artist. The relationship between the two letters is evident in the tonal value they both share (right).

Thomas Nozkowski
Untitled (7-22)
W
1993
oil on linen
22 x 28

Horizontal bands of dashed lines establish zones for the exhibition checklist. Each zone consists of three columns. The first is designated for the name of the artist and the title of the artwork, the second for the date and dimensions, and the third for a description of the medium and owner of the work. The unpretentious and straightforward organization of this information makes it easy to navigate. Dividing information into zoned bands such as this greatly improves the legibility of tabular data such as financial tables and scientific charts.

Typography possesses the power to raise ordinary ideas to kingly significance, and to lower significant ideas to trivia. In the catalog, information normally treated only as a side note is enlarged to fill an entire page. The size of the type, its color, and the unexpected surprise of seeing this mundane information at such a scale alters its importance (below).

Katherine Pavlis Porter *Tango for Daniel*	1990 80 1/2 x 113	oil on linen Courtesy of the artist
David Reed *No. 265*	1987-88 36 1/8 x 108 1/8	oil and alkyd on linen Hirshhorn Museum and Sculpture Garden, Smithsonian Institution, Washington, DC, Museum Purchase, 1989
David Reed *No. 279*	1987-89 108 x 48	oil and alkyd on linen Collection of Irv and Beth Robbins
David Reed *No. 308*	1991-92 28 x 112	oil and alkyd on linen Collection of Sue and David Workman
Robin Rose *State of Evaporation*	1993 3 panels, each 24 x 18	encaustic on linen on honeycomb aluminum panel Courtesy of the artist and M-13 Gallery, New York

dimensions are in inches, height precedes width precedes depth.

checklist

The computer provides an excellent tool for spontaneously manipulating and processing typographic elements by moving, sizing, and rotating them for effective compositions. This is evident in the design of the colophon page (below).

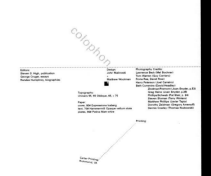

colophon

Editors:
Steven S. High, publication
George Cruger, essays
Randee Humphrey, biographies

Typography:
Univers 55, 55 Oblique, 65, + 75

Paper:
cover: 80# Expressions Iceberg
text, 70# Hammermill Opaque vellum slate
plates, 80# Patina Matt white

Design:
John Malinoski
+
Matthew Woolman

Photography Credits:
Lawrence Beck (Mel Bochner)
Tom Warren (Guy Corriero)
Fiona Rae, David Rose)
Harry Peterson (Joel Carreiro)
Beth Cummins (David Headley)
Zindman/Fremont (Joan Snyder, p.83)
Greg Heins (Joan Snyder, p.25)
Phillips/Schwab (Pat Steir, p. 24)
Steven Sloman (Terry Winters)
Matthew Phillips (Javier Tapia)
Dorothy Zeidman (Gregory Amenoff)
Dennis Cowley (Thomas Nozkowski)

Printing:

Carter Printing
Richmond, VA

Designer:
Peter Martin

atlas for a typeface exploration guides the reader on a meandering journey through uncommon and exotic typographic terrain. The landscape is characterized by universal attributes of typographic form: texture, rhythm, structure, kinetics, and tonality. Each of these attributes is further divided into visual qualities that aid in the exploration. For example, texture may be addressed in terms of smooth and rough or random and patterned. These typographic possibilities, referred to as a morphology, govern the design of the book and the experiments illustrated within. The sole typeface used for the investigations is New Baskerville; Univers functions as text. The book is not meant to be read from cover to cover, but to be entered and exited at any point along the way. All of the examples are computer-generated, providing ideas and inspiration.

The book's introduction offers intriguing advice – in the form of a typographic demonstration on how to use the book. The words *page* and *edge,* set in New Baskerville, are positioned vertically in a relationship revealing a mirror-image pattern of the letters *ge.* This pattern, which visually expresses the meaning of the accompanying text, grew from an awareness of the specific letters composing the two words, their spatial orientation, and the inherent qualities of the typeface used.

T E X T U R E
R H Y T H M
S T R U C T U R E
K I N E T I C S
T O N A L I T Y

paths of explorations found within morphological studies using various opposites to discover some visual abilities of a typeface called Baskerville

atlas for a typeface exploration

Every book must have an edge as does any exploration. But please remember that an edge is the same on both of its sides; it is not solely the end or the beginning. The edge is always an end of one and the beginning of another and vice versa. So let this page be simply an edge of this exploration and not its end or beginning.

The cover is a window providing the reader with a glimpse of what is to come. The explorations on the inside of the book are always the expression of opposites. For example, the five typographic principles listed on the cover form an orderly square shape in contrast to the adjacent configuration which is random and diffuse. Contrasts such as this are the basis of typographic communication. Dark is only dark in relation to light, etc. (above).

The elements used in the experiments are point, line, and plane, the underlying basis of all visual form. In typography, a point is understood as a dot or a single letter, a line as a rule line or a line of type, and a plane as a shape or a block of text type. Looking at type in this way acknowledges the fact that type is a visual as well as verbal communication medium, and that the visual attributes of type can affect a message's meaning.

a line is the extension of a point

a plane is an extension of a line
a plane is an extension of a line
a plane is an extension of a line
a plane is an extension of a line
a plane is an extension of a line
a plane is an extension of a line
a plane is an extension of a line
a plane is an extension of a line
a plane is an extension of a line
a plane is an extension of a line

plane
linear · non-linear
rhythm

On each spread, a key in the lower left-hand corner specifies the element and principle addressed in the accompanying experiment, as well as comparative oppositions illuminating the principle. The key to the left, for example, informs us that the element is a plane, the principle is rhythm, and the opposing themes are linear versus nonlinear.

Each spread consists of two typographic experiments, each demonstrating an opposing attribute of the assigned principle. A key to the experiments lies in the lower left-hand corner of the spread. When appropriate, a quote or statement explaining a principle or illuminating an experiment is found on the right-hand edge of the spread. Though the experiments are highly theoretical in nature, they provide the reader with many ideas for practical application. "Point" is expressed by both the dot

of an *i* with a smooth texture and the intersection of many lines of type crossing one another with a rough texture (top, right). "Line" is expressed as a single line of type with its inherent pattern of letters and as two flip-flopped and overlapping lines of type with a random texture (middle, right). "Line" is also expressed as an overlap of two text columns with a rough texture and two butted text columns with a smooth texture.

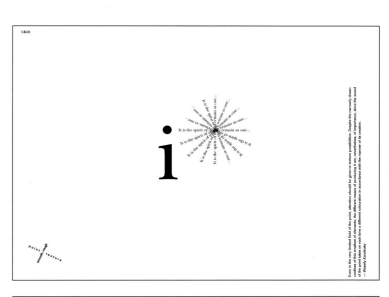

Representative spreads from *atlas for a typeface exploration* reveal a treasure chest of typographic possibilities. The first row of spreads represents explorations in point (letter); the second row reveals explorations in line; and the third row shows spreads devoted to plane (text block). The specific principles, elements, and opposing themes caption each example as follows:

[principle/element/opposing themes]

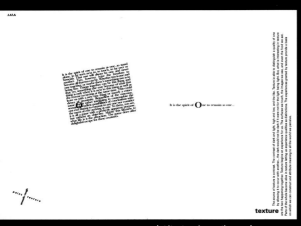

point/texture/smooth, rough

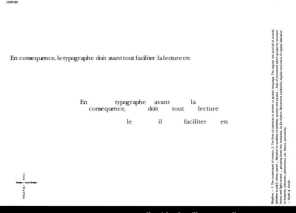

point/rhythm/repeating, contrasting

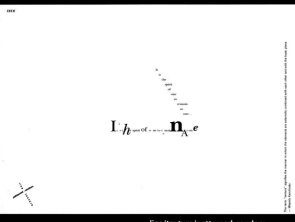

line/texture/patterned, random

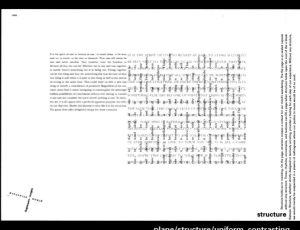

line/rhythm/linear, nonlinear

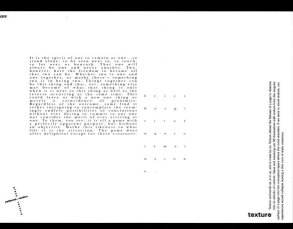

plane/texture/patterned, random

plane/structure/uniform, contrasting

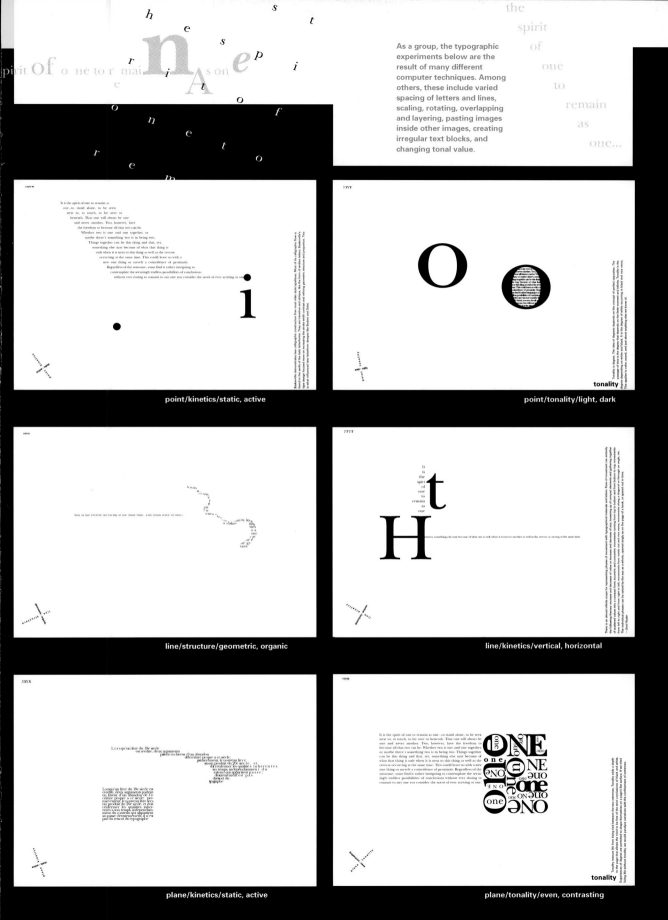

As a group, the typographic experiments below are the result of many different computer techniques. Among others, these include varied spacing of letters and lines, scaling, rotating, overlapping and layering, pasting images inside other images, creating irregular text blocks, and changing tonal value.

point/kinetics/static, active

point/tonality/light, dark

line/structure/geometric, organic

line/kinetics/vertical, horizontal

plane/kinetics/static, active

plane/tonality/even, contrasting

Roy Lichtenstein was a key player in establishing the Pop Art movement of the 1960s. This catalog is a record of the second retrospective exhibition held in his honor at New York's Guggenheim Museum. Typographically, the catalog is completely neutral, drawing absolutely no attention to itself. Its sole purpose is to accurately and objectively represent Lichtenstein and his work. Thomas James Cobden-Sanderson once stated, "The whole duty of typography, as with calligraphy, is to communicate to the imagination, without loss by the way, the thought or image intended to be communicated by the author." In this case, the validity and beauty of typography are judged on the basis of its ability to perform its duty. Certainly, expressive approaches to typography are desirable as circumstances permit. But here the typography is modest and stoic.

On the jacket, a detail of a Lichtenstein painting bleeds on all four sides. To preserve the integrity of this reproduction and to avoid any visual competition from the typography, the title of the book is not printed on top of the reproduction; rather, it is printed on a translucent sheet of paper that wraps around the book like a second jacket.

Set in Meta Caps and Bembo, the jacket type is integrated with the painting by aligning it to one of the painting's characteristic black lines, a major vertical line that divides the space in half.

Meta, a typeface designed by Eric Spiekermann, has been called the "Helvetica of the '90s." Originally designed for the German Post Office, it works best when set at text rather than display sizes. It is especially effective when set in small sizes on bad paper. The quirkiness of its design can be seen in the representative lower-case letters (right).

mn jf
u ec ag
t g
s

The energy and vitality of Lichtenstein's work is expressed through large, glamorous, full-color reproductions. These contrast greatly with the soft, gray text.

GIRLS, 1963–65

When working with typography, every detail, nuance, and refinement should be carefully considered. When you run across widows and orphans, for example, which awkwardly disrupt reading, eliminate them entirely. Sometimes, text must be rewritten to achieve this. Compare two text blocks, one with a nasty widow and one without.

When working with simple typography, every detail, nuance, and refinement should be carefully considered.

When working with simple typography, every detail, nuance, and refinement should be acknowledged.

When the *Brushstroke* paintings of 1965–66 were first exhibited, they were generally thought to be a comment on Abstract Expressionism. The artist admitted as much in interviews he gave at the time.[1] Lichtenstein's interpretation of the bravura brushstroke, replete with drips, seemed to be a hilarious spoof on the subject of the mannerisms of the New York School. Aesthetic issues of vital importance to artists such as de Kooning, Pollock, and Kline—gesture, and the involvement of the entire body in the act of painting, which Harold Rosenberg redefined as a spontaneous "action" or "event"— were reduced by Lichtenstein to the single brushstroke, which became the raison d'être for an entire series of paintings. In satirizing Abstract Expressionism by focusing on its characteristic brushstroke, Lichtenstein unlinked process (the action or event) and end-product (the record of that action or event) and thus diminished the ineffable mystery of artistic creation. His emphasis on one of the most obvious characteristics of New York School painting of the 1950s would seem to have summed up the objections to which he gave voice in his interview with Gene Swenson two years earlier.[2] Similarly, the fact that he singled out the drip, one of the most distinctive features of Action Painting, could be interpreted as a sly dig at the way in which an important component of an original painting style had been corrupted into an obligatory signature by lesser painters in the movement. Furthermore, *ARTnews* magazine was notorious for frequently emphasizing details of paintings in its pages during the 1950s, so much so that this emphasis lent itself to parody by artists less in thrall to the movement's mannerisms than its supporters realized. Generations of younger Abstract Expressionists also became known in the late 1950s for their slavish emulation of de Kooning's style of painting. Their pale imitation of his genius in capturing on canvas the spontaneous interaction between the painter and his innermost feelings could easily have induced Lichtenstein to reinterpret a style that had become a stereotype in the hands of less-capable artists.

Although there is a real connection between the *Brushstroke* paintings and Abstract Expressionism, the initial source for the series was a panel from the comic strip "The Painting" (fig. 127), in Charlton Comics' *Strange Suspense Stories*, no. 72 (October 1964).[3] *Brushstrokes* (fig. 126), 1965, is a direct reprise of that panel. In this painting, a hand holding a brush is situated at the lower-left corner of the canvas while above it to the right are a few bold horizontal and vertical strokes of paint and scattered drips. Lichtenstein liked the summary rendering of the hand holding the brush and the way in which the cartoonist indicated paint. From this image he developed a series of works that explored various aspects of painting, from the most basic house paint to the most esoteric commentary on the art of painting.

In a recent discussion, Lichtenstein stated that the overriding source for the *Brushstroke* series is the body of painterly painting from the Renaissance on.[4] Seventeenth-century Dutch portrait painter Frans Hals, whom Lichtenstein frequently mentions in this context, is a foremost example of a painterly painter, one whose extravagant brushwork is heir to a rich tradition in European art and an obvious precursor to the Abstract Expressionists' paintings. While Hals's painting technique was no more excessive than his gesticulating figures, it was his brushwork that interested Lichtenstein. Hals takes his place beside many other painters, both past and present, for whom the spontaneous gesture appears to be an end in and of itself.

127. Panel from "The Painting," in *Strange Suspense Stories*, no. 72 (October 1964). Charlton Comics.

left: **126. Roy Lichtenstein,** *Brushstrokes,* 1965. Oil and Magna on canvas, 121.9 x 121.9 cm (48 x 48 inches). Private collection.

The main text of this 12" x 12" book is set on a 36-pica measure in 12/16 Bembo. The text is unassuming and simple, giving center stage to the reproductions. With rare exception, the text is placed on the recto side of each spread in a single, very readable text block. Bembo works well as the main text because of its readability, and Meta Caps works well for titling and running heads because it possesses idiosyncratic qualities not unlike those in handwritten captions of comic strips. Shown here is a right-hand page.

Captions, set in 8/16 Bembo, unobtrusively identify the plates. Notice that the line spacing for the text and captions is the same, enabling them to be horizontally aligned.

Running heads and folios, set in Meta Caps, appear at the foot of the page.

The hypothesis that there is an ideally correct form for each letter of the alphabet is just as erroneous as Geofroy Tory's simple assumption that there is a relation between the shapes of letters and the human body; erroneous, because the shapes of letters have been in consistent process of modification from their very beginnings. Indeed, the shapes of letters now in daily use are due entirely to a convention, so that in preferring one form to another our only consideration need be for the conventions now existing and the degree in which each satisfies our sense of beauty. It should be kept clearly in mind that "the perfect model of a letter is altogether imaginary and arbitrary. There is a definite model for the human form. The painter, the sculptor, the architect, have their models in nature. The man who sets himself to make an alphabet has no copy except that left by former artists. . . . On all matters which pertain to the fashion of his letter he has no absolute stan-

The hypothesis that there is an ideally correct form for each letter of the alphabet is just as erroneous as Geofroy Tory's simple assumption that there is a relation between the shapes of letters and the human body; erroneous, because the shapes of letters have been in consistent process of modification from their very beginnings. Indeed, the shapes of letters now in daily use are due entirely to a convention, so that in preferring one form to another our only consideration need be for the conventions now existing and the degree in which each satisfies our sense of beauty. It should be kept clearly in mind that "the perfect model of a letter is altogether imaginary and arbitrary. There is a definite model for the human form. The painter, the sculptor, the architect, have their models in nature. The man who sets himself to make an alphabet has no copy except that left by former artists. . . . On all matters which pertain to the fashion of his letter he has no absolute stan-

The hypothesis that there is an ideally correct form for each letter of the alphabet is just as erroneous as Geofroy Tory's simple assumption that there is a relation between the shapes of letters and the human body; erroneous, because the shapes of letters have been in consistent process of modification from their very beginnings. Indeed, the shapes of letters now in daily use are due entirely to a convention, so that in preferring one form to another

When books are designed using a single text block on a page, it is important to consider how the text block activates the space. For example, if a text block is centered, the space is calm and reserved. If a block is positioned tightly against the edge of a page, tension is created and the page is energized. The size of a text block is also a factor. A small block may appear timid, a large block boisterous. It is the typographic grid that determines the actual proportions of text blocks.

Designer:
Takaaki Matsumoto

Reorientations: Looking East, an exhibition held at the Gallery at Takashimaya, New York, features three artists whose work draws upon the influences of Asian art and culture. The catalog for the exhibition, designed by Takaaki Matsumoto, emulates in design the Eastern theme of the exhibition. Matsumoto's exquisite and exotic use of materials, cultivated articulation of space and proportion, and fitting choice of typefaces provide a tangible and tactile artifact for gallery goers. In design, the catalog shares attributes of a Japanese poem: simple and concise in form and structure yet expansive in content.

The varied use of materials and typography is revealed in this open spread. The title page typography, printed on translucent paper, replicates the cover. Once the page is turned, the letters cast a visible shadow (above).

Four typefaces are used together in the catalog: Janson Text, City, Courier, and Meta. Janson is used for the interior text, City for titles and heads, Courier for front and back matter, and Meta for running heads and folios. It is interesting to compare the similarities and differences among these typefaces. The serifs of Courier and City behave similarly, though Courier is more rounded and City more squarish. The visual attributes of Janson and Meta contrast greatly with those of Courier and City (below).

This detail from an interview section of the catalog demonstrates an important principle that should always be considered: strive for obvious contrasts between typefaces that are assigned specific tasks within a publication (below, top), and avoid similar typefaces (below, bottom).

The cover typography is showcased on a strong and fibrous paper possessing a sensuous handmade quality. Embedded within its fibers are tidbits of discarded and recycled trash revealing jewel-like letterform fragments. The title of the catalog, silkscreened in yellow ink, is divided into four orderly lines. The word *Reorientations* comprises the first three of these lines, and is in a sense "reoriented" as a word on the page (above).

Janson Text
City
Courier
Meta

Kwon: The notion of exoticism in relation ways also operative now in relation to the of eco-consciousness, nature is also somet

Kwon: The notion of exoticism in relation ways also operative now in relation to the of eco-consciousness, nature is also somet

This specimen of Janson Text reveals why this typeface experiences continued popularity as a book face. A Dutch Old Style typeface, Janson exhibits excellent readability, a consistent texture, strong color, and spatial economy.

The way in which artists now incorporate or respond to the art and culture of different societies is equally varied. "Reorientations: Looking East" presents work by three American artists who have looked eastward; each draws from Asian art and/or culture the elements that are useful to them. In so doing, they illustrate a significant aspect of late twentieth-century Western art—the willingness and eagerness to go beyond the confines of a Greco-Roman heritage for inspiration. What makes the work of Ellen Brooks, Georgia Marsh, and Wade Saunders notable, in this regard, is how it manages to synthesize Asian influences with the artists' previous

INTRODUCTION

LYNN GUMPERT

As viewed from Europe in the second half of the nineteenth century, Japan epitomized a rare, unsullied exoticism, a country that was still primitive yet surprisingly sophisticated. Its long isolation from the West had protected it from the more negative aspects of an increasingly rapid industrialization. Japanese art and aesthetics, moreover, appeared to permeate the entire society, revealing an instinctive predilection for all that was deemed agreeable and, in particular, an innate respect for nature. The West was intrigued and enchanted; by 1872 the term *Japonisme* had been coined by a French critic to describe an immensely popular vogue for all things Japanese and the resulting impact on Western art.[1]

Certainly, a fascination with the exotic was an integral component of the romantic strain that infused the nineteenth century. Inextricably linked to both colonialism and an infatuation with all that was new, *Japonisme* can also be viewed as a product of what was then called "the Occident" and its larger attempt to differentiate itself from "the Orient." Orientalism, as writer and cultural critic Edward Said defines it, is an extensive and complex body of created theory and practice through which the West has attempted to demonstrate its superiority over the East.[2] Upon closer analysis, concepts like Orientalism and *Japonisme* have more to do with Western society and culture than with any "true" notions about Asia.

As André Gide once put it, "Influence creates nothing, it reawakens — the power of an influence lies not in what it makes but in revealing some part of me yet unknown to myself."[3] Those who depict or characterize foreign cultures often reveal more about themselves and their reveries than about the societies they attempt to define. A more recent analysis of Japan as the most exemplary of postmodern societies, the "paradigm of free-floating signs, artifice, cultural clichés and coded representations," can be seen as an updated variant — although simultaneously more self-conscious and more self-critical — of Orientalism in its broadest sense.[4] At the same time, this characterization also conveys the dramatic extent to which Western views of the Far East have changed over the course of the twentieth century. Now, on the brink of the twenty-first century, the impact and influence of Asian art and culture continues, but it is more diversified than ever before.

The way in which artists now incorporate or respond to the art and culture of different societies is equally varied. "Reorientations: Looking East" presents work by three American artists who have looked eastward; each draws from Asian art and/or culture the elements that are useful to them. In so doing, they illustrate a significant aspect of late twentieth-century Western art — the willingness and eagerness to go beyond the confines of a Greco-Roman heritage for inspiration. What makes the work of Ellen Brooks, Georgia Marsh, and Wade Saunders notable, in this regard, is how it manages to synthesize Asian influences with the artists' previous concerns. The resulting works of art are extremely compelling, at once reassuringly familiar and strangely disconcerting.

For Georgia Marsh, it is not only the visual art of the Far East — most specifically that of Japan and China — that has interested her but its literature as

Designer:
Philip B. Meggs

This museum catalog presents the life and work of Tomás Gonda, a Hungarian graphic designer whose work reflected the minimal nuances of color, light, and form. Gonda was a functionalist who despised decorative design and superfluous form. His typographic design reflected a concern for clear and precise communication. These concerns were also at the root of the famous Ulm School of Design in Germany, where Gonda taught for a time. Most often, he used sans serif types such as Helvetica, for to him, these represented the ideals of modern culture. Always, Gonda attempted to strip messages to their bare essence. This catalog reflects Gonda's minimalist concerns; it is straightforward, simple, and direct. In a sense also, it is a celebration of Helvetica, the typeface that has become a household word since the desktop publishing explosion.

The square proportions of the catalog cover are echoed by two overlapping squares rotated 45°. The square, a design motif often used in Tomás Gonda's work, reappears as a central design motif in the catalog. The linear color blend found in the squares is reminiscent of Gondas's use of color. It is achieved by simply selecting two colors and telling the computer to blend them into a gradation. Most design and page-layout software enables you to achieve this simple but colorful effect.

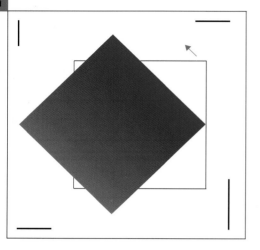

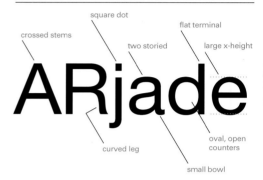

square dot
flat terminal
crossed stems
two storied
large x-height

ARjade

curved leg
oval, open counters
small bowl

Helvetica is the workhorse of typefaces. Clean, simple, and direct, it remains one of the most popular typefaces of all time. This version of Helvetica is based on a numerical system of weights and widths very similar to that of Univers. Helvetica provides a family of typefaces ranging from razor-blade thin (Neue Helvetica 35) to buxom (Neue Helvetica 95) variations. Each variation within the typeface family is amazingly compatible with the others, providing a high degree of visual unity for any publication. This quality is craftily demonstrated in this catalog design. This diagram displays some of Helvetica's more noticeable traits.

A **Life** in Design

95	85	75	65	55	45
black	heavy	bold	medium	roman	light

The catalog title on the cover is composed of six different weights of Helvetica (indicated above by the blue dotted lines). The effect of this mixture is a visual gradation of type that complements the color blend of the square. The title also demonstrates the versatility of Helvetica as a type family. This full complement of weights can be used interchangeably, and there is never a question that they are from the same family. The many weights can be used together in any combination for emphasis and contrast. The computer enabled the designer to experiment with several typographic dark-to-light themes. The variation shown to the right is used on the catalog's foreword page.

Massimo Vignelli

On the foreword page, three columns of text type set respectively in three weights of Helvetica, 45 Light, 55 Roman, and 65 Medium (below and opposite), establish yet another variation on the catalog's gradational theme. Notice how as the weight of the text blocks gets heavier, the tone of the type becomes darker. This darkening occurs because as the strokes in the letters thicken, the counterforms shrink.

Before and during the sixties, but not after, graphic designers were seriously striving to establish graphic design as not only a profession, but a deeply committed one as well. The School of Ulm was the heart of the movement. There, communication design (as it was called, rather than graphic design) had a real function in society and its production process. Nothing could have been more remote from "commercial arts" than the Ulm attitude.

Tomás Gonda grew up in that matrix, with love and dedication toward his profession, with hate and contempt for the so-called

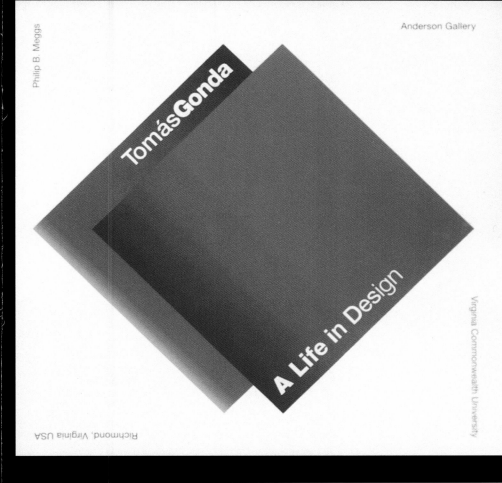

Tomás Gonda

A Life in Design

Richmond, Virginia USA

Virginia Commonwealth University

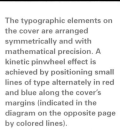

The typographic elements on the cover are arranged symmetrically and with mathematical precision. A kinetic pinwheel effect is achieved by positioning small lines of type alternately in red and blue along the cover's margins (indicated in the diagram on the opposite page by colored lines).

Usually, medium-weight text types, as the Helvetica Roman below, are the easiest to read. They possess excellent balance between the thickness of the strokes and the size of the counters.

Most desktop publishing systems enable you to select a "bold" option for type under the Style menu. It is far better, however, to select the specially-drawn weight variants of a type family, for these are drawn with specific

proportions in mind. Choosing "bold" under the style menu obviously makes letters bolder, but the intended proportions of the typeface are distorted.

The foreword for this book was written by Massimo Vignelli.

commercial art which was pervading the American scene. Over here, he was working like a missionary, and it was appropriate that we would occasionally work together. We shared the commitment and the desire to raise the level of communication design, stamp out silly graphics from products and relegate it to cheap art galleries where it belongs. Tomás' work was to the point, understated when appropriate, overstated when needed. His talent and elegance were expressed through his work, the careful handling of the typography, the meaningful use of color as opposed to the prevailing indiscriminate use of it.

Working with him, one learned the relative importance of graphic design in the world context. His intelligence would always lower your ego to reasonable levels. After all, design is only the solution to a problem, not ART. What makes the solution interesting is the amount of intelligence in it and its ability to transform the mundane into the sublime. Tomás Gonda knew all this and, as a designer, as a teacher, and as a friend, he always made sure you understood where the boundary of design stands.

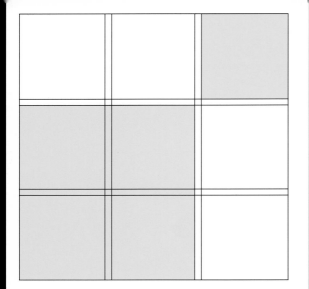

Before and during the sixties, but not after, graphic designers were seriously striving to establish not only graphic design as a profession, but a deeply committed one as well. The School of Ulm was the heart of the movement. There, communication design (as it was called, rather than graphic design) had a real function in society and its production process. Nothing could have been more remote from "commercial arts" than the Ulm attitude.

Tomás Gonda grew up in that matrix, with love and dedication toward his profession, with hate and contempt for the so-called commercial art which was pervading the American scene. Over here, he was working like a missionary, and it was appropriate that we would occasionally work together. We shared the commitment and the desire to raise the level of communication design, stamp out silly graphics from products and relegate it to cheap art galleries where it belongs. Tomás' work was to the point, understated when appropriate, overstated when needed. His talent and elegance were expressed through his work, the careful handling of the typography, the meaningful use of color as opposed to the prevailing indiscriminate use of it.

Working with him, one learned the relative importance of graphic design in the world context. His intelligence would always lower your ego to reasonable levels. After all, design is only the solution to a problem, not ART. What makes the solution interesting is the amount of intelligence in it and its ability to transform the mundane into the sublime. Tomás Gonda knew all this and, as a designer, as a teacher, and as a friend, he always made sure you understood where the boundary of design stands.

Foreword

Massimo Vignelli

7

Tomás Gonda placed emphasis on mathematical order in his graphic design. He relied on strict grid systems such as the one used by the designer for the design of this 8.5"x 8.5" catalog. As shown above, this is a three-column grid composed of 14.5 pica columns with 1 pica separating the columns. Vertical divisions are also employed that aid in the placement of photographic and illustrative material. The margin measurements are three picas on the top and outside, and four picas inside and at the bottom. Indicated by the yellow shapes, the grid is used flexibly, with type units and images occupying as few as one column or as many as three. A typographic grid provides an invisible framework for organizing all of the parts of a publication.

A typographic grid need not be a straightjacket. Violating them in an appropriate way can bring visual variety and interest to a publication. Violating a grid does not mean that some elements run out of control like a herd of buffalo, having no relationhip to the rest of the publication. Elements should always relate visually to other elements within the publication. For example, on this page the subhead *foreword* and name of the author violate the three-column grid but echo the recurring diamond shape, indicated by the blue-dotted line. Typographic components throughout the catalog that ignore the three-column grid are positioned on the diamond for a unified appearance.

Within any publication there exists a need to provide visual unity from page to page. If all the pages look exactly the same, however, the publication lacks variety and is boring. If each page is composed without the others in mind, chaos threatens any cohesiveness between them. The two pages to the right possess both similarities and differences. The diamond motif and centrally located black rectangle with reversed type are visual themes that tie the pages together, yet on each they are used differently for variety.

Life without **industry** is guilt,

and **industry** without **art**

is **brutality.**

— John Ruskin

In typography, contrast has a twofold purpose: it helps the reader determine the relative importance of various parts within the message, and it provides the page with dynamic visual rhythm. Typographic contrasts of size, tone, color, texture, direction, weight, and width (to name a few) can effectively be incorporated into the page. The more distinct the contrasts the better. If the reader cannot easily distinguish between typographical elements such as heads, subheads, and text, information is difficult to navigate. In making contrasts, use as few typographic variants as possible. In other words, if you can say it with one face, one size, and two weights of type, why use a second size? More variations only complicate the message and clutter the page. The quote above appears opposite the title page in the book. Contrast is exhibited through a weight change in key words. Notice also how the type visually sparkles. To the right is the same quote, void of contrasting words and lackluster in appearance.

Life without

industry is guilt,

and industry without art

is brutality.

— John Ruskin

On the title page of the catalog, the name *Gonda* is reversed out of a black rectangle to appear as white, creating a dominant typographic element. Three of the letters merge with the white background, adding to the dynamics of the title (first column, top). Without changing the size of the word or the rectangle, many other computer transformations are possible. Merely changing colors, moving letters up and down within the rectangle, and altering the weights of certain letters create a wide range of visual possibilities. When your message's content calls for a typographic manipulation such as this, remember that the most effective results emerge from the interplay of simple forms and devices.

Typographic Specimens: The Great Typefaces presents 38 of the finest type families in the world with a chapter devoted to each family. A visually neutral typeface was needed to present these families, one with no visual affectations or awkward quirks. Univers was chosen for this task, for it is a type design whose visual presence is purely objective and anonymous. The focal point of the book is a large Univers *T*. This letterform provides the proportions for the underlying typographical structure of the book. Each chapter commences with a concise sketch of the family's history, set in a representative typeface from the family. Complete fonts of each family are presented in both text and display type, and all of the specimens are available for use in desktop publishing. The design of the book provides a guide for the comparison, study, and selection of typefaces.

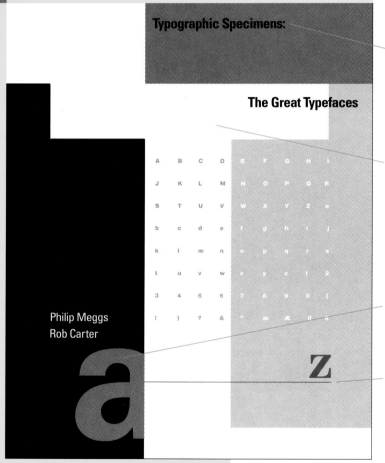

Typographic Specimens:

The Great Typefaces

Philip Meggs
Rob Carter

Thinking of a cover as an entranceway into the interior of a publication, just as a door is an entranceway into a building, will aid you in your own cover designs. A cover can describe a publication's structure, and inform readers about what to expect on the inside.

The book's title, subtitle, and author credits are all set in Univers 66 at the same size – 24-point – for visual consistency. A weight contrast alone is enough to distinguish these elements. Chapter heads on the inside of the book appear in the same size and position.

A large upper-case Univers *T* dominates the cover of the book, and becomes the book design's primary visual theme. This form is found again in different variations on the division pages. The *T* was created by positioning three rectilinear shapes on the computer screen. The space between the shapes (the negative space) establishes the letter.

The lower-case *a* "sent to the back" by the computer peeks at the reader from within the black shape, creating an illusion of three-dimensional space.

A horizontal rule aligned with the curved stroke of the lower-case *a* underscores the alphabet appearing above it as a square pattern.

Univers is a type family of great versatility. A range of the various weights and widths representing the family are shown below.

a Univers 49

a Univers 59

a Univers 67

a Univers 55

a Univers 65

a Univers 75

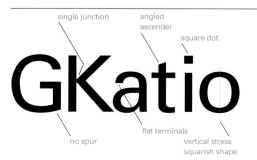

single junction
angled ascender
square dot

GKatio

no spur
flat terminals
vertical stress
squarish shape

Univers, designed by Adrian Frutiger in 1957, is a sans serif family based on a numerical coding system to identify weight and width variations within the family. It has remained over the years one of the most versatile families, where due to unified design, fonts can be freely mixed. Shown here is the book-weight Univers 55.

Design: **John T. Drew**

Univers was designed in 1957 by Adrian Frutiger. Relying upon Swiss objectivity, he used a numerical coding system for the twenty-one-member Univers family as a means to clearly distinguish one variation from another and to avoid the confusing descriptions normally found in the industry, such as light, regular, demi, bold, etc. The first digit in each font's number refers to stroke weight, three being the lightest and eight the heaviest. The second digit refers to the width of the letters, revealing expanded and condensed forms. Roman fonts are assigned odd numbers and italics are assigned even numbers. Univers 55 is the book weight and the source from which all other designs were developed. Frutiger intended the variations within the family to be used interchangeably; he carefully balanced the need for unity as well as diversity within the system.

With the design of Univers, Frutiger initiated a trend toward larger x-heights. All strokes within each letter contrast in width only slightly, but the severe geometry of the modern sans serif was replaced with optical subtlety. Other distinguishing characteristics include flat terminals in letters such as **a**, **c**, and **e**; slightly squared appearance as seen in the letter **O**; square dots on the **i** and **j**; and an angled ascender on the **t**. The arm and leg of the **K** join at a single junction, and the **G** does not have a spur.

Frutiger removed from Univers most of the quirky features of the traditional grotesque face and came up with a very legible text and display face. Univers continues to be widely used in signage because of its simplicity and clarity. As a sans-serif text face, it rivals some of the most frequently used serif faces for readability.

Specimens are set in **Linotype Univers**

Univers 55

abcdefghijklmnopqrstuvwxyz
ABCDEFGHIJKLMNOPQRSTUVWXYZ
$&1234567890(.,""";:!?)

abcdefghijklmno
pqrstuvwxyzAB
CDEFGHIJKLMN
OPQRSTUVWX
YZ$&123456789
0(.,"";:!?)

abcdefghijklmnopqrstuvwxyz
ABCDEFGHIJKLMNOPQRSTUV
WXYZ$&1234567890(.,"";:!?)

The top example details a text block located at the beginning of a chapter. Here, Univers 55 provides effective readability due to the addition of 3 points between lines. Generally speaking, sans serif typefaces with large x-heights require at least 2 points of space between lines for comfortable reading. Compare this with the bottom example where 9-point Univers 55 is set solid.

With the design of Univers, Frutiger initiated a trend toward larger x-heights. All strokes within each letter contrast in width only slightly, but the severe geometry of the modern sans serif was replaced with optical subtlety. Other distinguishing characteristics

With the design of Univers, Frutiger initiated a trend toward larger x-heights. All strokes within each letter contrast in width only slightly, but the severe geometry of the modern sans serif was replaced with optical subtlety. Other distinguishing characteristics include flat terminals

The simple procedure of combining two lines with a small black rectangle effectively creates typographic markers that identify sizes of type throughout the book. Point sizes appear as white numerals in small black rectangles. The computer readily enables designers to create useful configurations such as this. A few variations on this idea that can be easily made with the computer are illustrated below.

72

72

72

72

Designers:
Craig Minor
Cheryl Brzezinski-Beckett

This wedding invitation in the form of a small booklet uses type and image to juxtapose the male themes *science* and *build* with the female themes *art* and *nurture*. Several typefaces are implemented, including Helvetica Inserat, Teknik and Orator for the male, and Minion, New Baskerville and Ribbon 131 for the female. The male themes appear on the left-hand pages; the female themes on the right-hand pages. Images join the type to reinforce the themes. For example, a carpenter's plane pairs with *build,* while a rose completes the idea of *nurture*. At the end of the booklet, the male and female parts share the same pages for a "marriage" of oppositional themes.

This delicate booklet is organized by centering selected typographic elements and images along a centered horizontal axis (indicated by the blue dotted line). This symmetry is very relaxed, with some images such as the swirling *S* asymmetrically positioned to prevent the pages from becoming too rigid. Pictured here is the first page of the booklet where the *HE/SHE* theme begins. An elegant hand-drawn *S* is combined with Mona Lisa Recut letters to join the words *HE* and *SHE*.

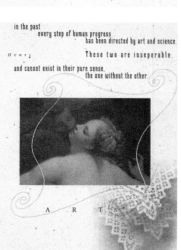

Type and image often support each other in a relationship called a word/image pairing. In this example, a scientific drawing of a human heart pairs with the word *SCIENCE* for a more intensified meaning. Note also that the word is set in Orator, a mechanical face, and enclosed in brackets that identify it as a scientific fact.

[S C I E N C E]

The last page of the invitation booklet presents the wedding announcement. In contrast to earlier pages, and bearing in mind the solemn occasion, this page assumes a formal, traditional quality through its centered typography. Note the generous spaces separating the parts of the announcement. This enables readers to easily negotiate the information established in the three critical parts of the message: who is being married, when it will happen, and where it will take place. The names of the bride and groom appear with very wide letter spacing for emphasis. The word *US* overlapping the word *to* symbolically represents the marriage union.

Mr. and Mrs. Walter Brzezinski
request the honor
of your presence
at the marriage of their daughter

Cheryl Ann Brzezinski

to

Dr. Philip Ronald Beckett

{ *Friday, May 20, 1994*

at 5:30 pm
at St. Basil's Church
South Haven, Michigan
reception immediately following at
The Landmark Center, St. Joseph, Michigan

confluence

harmony

resonance

To live between the opposites,
we stretch out our arms   and   push them as far apart as we can
and then live
in the resonating
      s p a c e
            between
                  them

b l y

in the past
      every step of human progress
            has been directed by art and science.
Henri
            These two are inseparable,

and cannot exist in their pure sense,
            the one without the other.

As demonstrated in quotations sprinkled throughout the pages, lines of type can be organized for poetic effect. Line breaks emphasize how the text might be read, and varied spacing between letters and words indicate pauses in reading. As spaces increase in size, pauses increase in duration.

If you want to combine different typefaces in design, make sure you use those that look very different from one another. This precaution will ensure that no ambiguity exists in the function of each typeface used. The use of two similar serif typefaces, for example, does not provide enough contrast to ensure that the reader will perceive the difference between them. Here, the word *fire* set in Ribbon 131 not only connotes the idea of fire because of its flamelike quality, it also stands apart visually from the word *sun*, set in Teknik; there is no ambiguity in the combination of these two typefaces.

SCIENCE   art

WATER   fire

BUILD   nurture

Type is words made visible, and the visual traits of typefaces can imply specific meanings. When you are selecting typefaces, try to identify those with a visual form and design relating to the inherent meaning of the words. Sometimes this verbal/visual equation is very subtle. A detail from one of the pages provides an excellent example of how letters, due to their intrinsic visual qualities, reinforce the meanings of the words they represent. The geometric, blocky qualities of Orator (left), represent masculine qualities; the familiar friendliness of Minion (right) portrays the feminine side.

f i r e

s u n

Designers:
**Craig Minor
Cheryl Brzezinski-
Beckett**

Solutions to typographic problems are often embedded in the message's content. For this exhibition catalog on architecture, furniture, interior and urban design, the designers represent in the typography and layout the unique qualities of blueprints. This gives the reader a sense of the planning processes involved in each of the exhibition areas. Orator, the primary type-face chosen for this project is a geometric, mono-stroke face consisting entirely of capital letters. The visual qualities of the face remind one of the hand lettering used on blueprints. To further the blueprint theme, type and images appear in blueprint blue ink.

Each page of the book is divided into two columns. You can see in the diagram that the text and images occupy the same space as determined by the width of the columns. Heads are centered above text blocks and images for a very formal look. In addition, the text blocks are set justified for a square finish, a trait that further links the text and images together.

In contrast to the symmetrical pages of the catalog, asymmetrical text type configurations alluding to architectural structures provide variety. The blue outline reveals the shape of a "built" text block.

Above, serving as a running head and a device to separate information about the catalog's featured design offices, the flip-flopped words, *Best Laid Plans*, provide the illusion of reading from the back of architectural plans. This is accomplished by using a "flip horizontal" command. This simple computer manipulation cleverly extends the blueprint metaphor.

Text can be flipped in four ways: normal, flipped horizontally, flipped horizontally and vertically, flipped vertically (from top to bottom, right).

type
type
type
type

BEST LAID PLANS

ARCHITECTURE . COMPETITIONS .
INTERIOR ARCHITECTURE . URBAN
DESIGN . FURNITURE DESIGN .

The catalog cover consists of a large photograph of architectural plans with the Orator title, *Best Laid Plans*, reversed from the photograph and overprinted in yellow. The lower section of the cover, set in widely spaced Orator letters, announces the catalog's contents. Bullets separate these units of information.

Setting text in all capital letters is normally not recommended because it is more difficult to read than text set with capitals and/or lowercase letters. But when you find an occasion to use all capitals, as here, readability can be improved by adding adequate space between the lines. This is particularly true of Orator, a typeface that has loose letter and word spacing when set normally. The top example is text as it appears in the catalog: 9.75/13. The bottom example, set 9.75/9.75 is difficult to read because line spacing appears smaller than wordspacing; the eye has difficulty distinguishing between lines.

IF THIS SHOW HAD BEEN HELD 10 YEARS AGO, IT MIGHT HAVE CONSISTED LARGELY OF SPECULATIVE OFFICE BUILDINGS WITH SLICK GLASS SKINS AND POSTMODERN PEDIMENTS. WHEN I PREVIEWED THE BOARDS FOR THIS SHOW, HOWEVER, I COUNTED ONLY FOUR OFFICE BUILDINGS - ONE IN FLORIDA, ONE IN BOSTON, AND TWO IN HOUSTON. IN FACT, BETTER THAN TWO-THIRDS OF THE BOARDS SHOWED HOUSES, EITHER BUILT OR UNBUILT, RANGING IN STYLE FROM POLEMICAL MODERNISM TO ACADEMICALLY CORRECT HISTORICISM TO THE UNCOM-FORTABLY HYBRIDIZED DESIGN LANGUAGE OF SUBURBAN

IF THIS SHOW HAD BEEN HELD 10 YEARS AGO, IT MIGHT HAVE CONSISTED LARGELY OF SPECULATIVE OFFICE BUILDINGS WITH SLICK GLASS SKINS AND POSTMODERN PEDIMENTS. WHEN I PREVIEWED THE BOARDS FOR THIS SHOW, HOWEVER, I COUNTED ONLY FOUR OFFICE BUILDINGS - ONE IN FLORIDA, ONE IN BOSTON, AND TWO IN HOUSTON. IN FACT, BETTER THAN TWO-THIRDS OF THE BOARDS SHOWED HOUSES, EITHER BUILT OR UNBUILT, RANGING IN STYLE FROM POLEMICAL MODERNISM TO ACADEMICALLY CORRECT HISTORICISM TO THE UNCOM-FORTABLY HYBRIDIZED DESIGN LANGUAGE OF SUBURBAN

IF THIS SHOW HAD BEEN HELD 10 YEARS AGO, IT MIGHT HAVE

IF THIS SHOW HAD BEEN HELD 10 YEARS AGO, IT MIGHT HAVE

IF THIS SHOW HAD BEEN HELD 10 YEARS AGO, IT MIGHT HAVE

In addition to selecting line spacing, you may also determine the spaces for letters and words. Letter, word, and line spacing should be considered in relationship to one another: tight word and line spacing with tight letter spacing, and loose word and line spacing with loose letter spacing. Orator with normal letter and word spacing (top), with 50% word spacing (middle), and with 25% word spacing (bottom). In the bottom example, words bump into each other, sacrificing readability.

In the book *Espresso*, photographs and type engage in visual conversation, while readers seduced into the pages learn of the history and rituals associated with this celebrated beverage. Bodoni Book serves as the main text face, a fitting choice for a subject that shares the same Italian heritage. Bodoni's crisp forms complement dreamy café images, while the dignified, all-capitals Orator serves to represent quoted material.

Often, type overlaps image, appearing as though it hovers inches above the surface of the page. The typography ranges from very subtle and quiet to dynamic and tactile. Always controlled and never distracting, it remains readable and inviting.

Expressive variations of the cover title are exhibited in the chapter division spreads. The word *morning,* for example, which is paired with a photograph of alarm clocks, also reads as *ring* due to the enlargement of the letters *r* and *g.* Time to wake up for a cup of java (above)!

IT WAS A PLEASA

CAFÉ, WARM A

CLEAN AND FRIENDL

AND I HUNG UP

OLD WATERPROOF

THE COAT RACK

DE A S WO

AND WEATHERED FE

HAT ON THE RA

ABOVE THE BEN

AND ORDERED A

On the cover, a soft, black and white photograph of informally stacked dishes contrasts with the formal, right-angled arrangement of the title and subtitle typography. Note the alignment of the letter spaced subtitle, *CULTURE & CUISINE* with the descender of the lower-case *p* in the title *Espresso.* This relationship brings order to the typography and dynamic visual flare to the cover (above).

Helvetica Black letters of varying size, and the repetition of the three lower-case *s* letters, lend energy to the animated title, *Expresso.* In addition, the eye-catching lower-case *r,* printed in an espresso-like color, provides the type with an alluring aromatic quality (above).

ESPRESSO

CULTURE & CUISINE

BY

KARL PETZKE AND

SARA SLAVIN

Photography: Karl Petzke

Art Direction / Styling: Sara Slavin

Text: Carolyn Miller

Design: Jennifer Morla

Food: Sandra Cook

CHRONICLE BOOKS
SAN FRANCISCO

The title page sparkles like a starlit night, and the brilliant typographic pattern reminds one of a constellation. Type reversed from a black background achieves a luminescent and resonant quality, offering a respite from the normal black-on-white reading experience (above). Reversing type works well for this title page, as it contains only a small amount of type. But large amounts of reversed text suffer in readability due to the vibrating, dazzling contrast between the letters and their background. Reversed type should be used with discretion.

Part of the appeal of coffee is that it is a drink that marks the transitions in our day: the transition from sleeping to waking, from work to rest, from day to night. It marks the end of meals and the end of solitude, and accompanies us through the day like a talisman of both change and continuity.

❧

Rumi was a thirteenth-century Sufi who wrote radiant poems of spiritual longing and mystical transformation. He was also the founder of the order of the whirling dervishes. Before coffee was adopted by the masses, it was the ritual drink of priests and acolytes, who used it as an aid to meditation and prayer. We like to think of Rumi whirling and whirling for hours in his sky blue Sufi robes, transported to another reality by constant movement and many tiny cups of ceremonially brewed coffee, the patron dervish of all future coffeehouse poets.

Existentialism, feminism, and the modern novel were all partly shaped in the cafés of Paris. Jean-Paul Sartre and Simone de Beauvoir first wrote in Le Dôme until it was taken over by German soldiers in 1940, at which time they moved to Café de Flore.

❧

One of the oldest European coffeehouses, Caffè Greco in Rome was founded sometime before 1750. A popular stop on the Grand Tour, it has hosted some of the greatest writers and musicians of Western civilization. Caffè Greco is located on Via Condotti at the foot of the Spanish Steps.

Each page in this visually romantic book carefully balances diverse typographic elements with the aid of a two-column grid. The example to the left demonstrates the grid's use.

The text is set in justified 10/16 Bodoni Book. Columns are 12 picas in width, with an interval of 2.25 picas between them. The plentiful space between lines provides the text with exceptional readability.

A thin, vertical ruled line separates the two text columns, which in relationship to each other are staggered vertically on the page.

Fleurons clearly mark the division between one section of text and another.

Ample white space contributes to the book's polish, luxuriousness, and relaxed quality. The reader feels comfortable in moving slowly and meditatively through the pages.

The book celebrates espresso with both color and black and white photographs of café scenes, and typography given tailored attention to detail. These representative spreads demonstrate the visual variety that can be achieved with a basic 2-column grid and a sense of visual rhythm and pacing (above and right).

A quote set in Orator, printed over a warm café image, and extending across an entire spread creates a transparent, three-dimensional effect and a venetian blind of type through which the reader peers (below).

When printing type over a photograph or other image, as shown here, it is important to have sufficient contrast between them. Readability is greatly diminished when type and its background are too similar in tone and/or color.

THE ITALIANS KNOW THAT COUNTRY IS ... IMBUED KNOW THAT THERE IS DISTINGUISH OR TO SMILE ON THE FACE OF DONATELLO'S SAN GIOR- WORKS OF ART, THE HAPPY' AND OF MAKING AN ART WHICH EMBRACES OTHERS IN ITALY, THE ING, BUT WHICH CAN MASTERED, THE ART OF EVERYTHING IN THEIR WITH THEIR SPIRIT, THEY NO NEED, REALLY, TO CHOOSE BETWEEN THE A *CAMERIERE* AND GIO.... THEY ARE ALL 'GREAT ART OF BEING OTHER PEOPLE HAPPY, AND INSPIRES A ONLY ART WORTH LEARN- NEVER BE REALLY INHABITING THE EARTH.

LUIGI BARZINI, *THE ITALIANS*

Designer:
Christopher Ozubko

For this guide to finding performance space in the Seattle, Washington, area, the typeface Humanist 521 plays the lead role, with Modula and Matrix in supporting parts. Humanist sans serif typefaces owe their origins to classical Roman letterforms based on handwriting of the 15th century. Sufficiently living up to its name, Humanist 521 possesses a distinctive handwritten appearance due to its excellent readability and efficient flexibility of weights and widths. The *Space Finder* surely benefits from this typeface, for it enlivens dull and repetitive information composed of lists and indexes. Images, color, and texture are added to the typography for a dynamic and inviting guide.

This diagram of the book jacket illustrates the integration of type into the front cover, back cover, and flaps. The designer used several computer effects, including overlapping letters, words exceeding the boundaries of the cover, and contrasting colors. The jacket reveals an intriguing space, a convincing visual metaphor that relates to the guide's purpose.

Much of the information in this booklet takes the form of tabular data. This is consistently organized into a two-column grid (indicated by the blue-dotted lines) with 1 pica separating columns. The 9-point Humanist 521 type is composed of lines separated with five points of lead. This is adequate space between the lines to easily guide the eye from one data entry to another. The bottom example shows what happens to readability when lines are set solid. The eye finds it difficult to negotiate the information, for the crowded lines lack separation and distinction.

SOUND

Microphones:	1
Intercom system:	Yes
Facility acoustics:	Fair

OTHER STAGE EQUIPMENT

Projection screen(s):	1
Screen size:	15' x 15'
Stage masking:	Curtains side-to-side, back curtain

Kane Hall

UW, DG-10

Seattle, WA 98195

Booking:	Staff, 543-2985
Manager:	Donald Zongker, 543-9903
Owner:	University of Washington

SOUND

Microphones:	1
Intercom system:	Yes
Facility acoustics:	Fair

OTHER STAGE EQUIPMENT

Projection screen(s):	1
Screen size:	15' x 15'
Stage masking:	Curtains side-to-side, back curtain

Irregular geometric shapes serve as backgrounds for subheads and other supporting information. The procedure for making these cut-out shapes involves creating rectangles, reversing type from the rectangles and then "notching" the rectangles with rectilinear shapes (indicated in gray). The lengths of the lines of type dictate the specific shapes of the backgrounds. This method affords an infinite variety of possibilities and infuses the type with visual interest and emphasis.

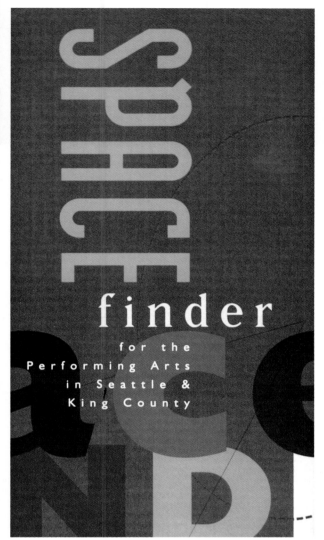

SPACE finder

for the Performing Arts in Seattle & King County

1,001+ seats

The cover visually suggests the content of the booklet, with letterforms of varying colors overlapping one another as if floating in space. Such effects are relatively easy to obtain with a computer: simply drag the letters until they overlap and then "send" the appropriate letters to the back. The difficult part of this exercise lies in positioning the letterforms in the space. Typographic composition requires sensitivity and practice.

The booklet's division pages combine old engravings, silhouettes, textures, and shapes into sensuous visual environments. Large type, reversed and appearing as the color of the paper, clearly marks the beginning of each new section.

Subheads within the tabular settings appear in outlined boxes created with an orthogonal line tool. This is a simple but effective way to create emphasis for the quick identification of elements (top). Possibilities for other variations on this theme are endless, just a few of which are shown here.

SOUND

SOUND

SOUND

SOUND

SOUND

SOUND

British novelist Virginia Woolf's *A Room of One's Own* is one in a series of limited-edition books published by the Heritage Press in Dallas, Texas. Each year, a well-known designer is asked to design a book. Showcasing the high quality of the press and the traditions of fine bookmaking, the books are provided as gifts to friends and potential clients of the press. Perhaps the most striking aspect of this book is the hand-lettered type by the book's designer, Paula Scher. Paula is well known for her inventive use of eccentric and historic typefaces, and the stunning letters drawn by computer for this book are consistent with her typographic approach. These letters reflect the visual ambience of the late 1920s, the period in which the book was written, but also have relevance in the typographic arena of today.

Echoing the cover, the title page is a variation on a typographic theme. Similarities and differences establish both unity and variety – pleasant and desired traits of any book design. Eliminating the toned fill of the overlaps, changing the color, and adding an alternative title treatment distinguish the title page from the cover.

On the cover, the author's name, composed of sleek geometric letters of a silver hue, push against the margins and illuminate the black background. Tightly spaced horizontal lines creating a toned fill are applied to counterforms and the spaces of the overlapping letters. The effect is a melodious interplay of line and plane. The two overlapping letters *O* establish a point of focus, and the space beneath them is a comfortable habitat for the date. Part of the appeal of these letters are the thinness and delicacy of their strokes.

The letterforms are constructed of thin horizontal, vertical, diagonal, and circular lines. These basic elements are easily produced by the computer, but a trained eye and empathic response to typographic space and proportion are required to organize them into an effective composition. The words share a common baseline and capline; the overlapping letters *O*, and the convergent strokes of letters *R* and *W*, and *A* and *F* contribute to the visual effect. It is reasonable to conclude that the overlapping letters connote the stream-of-consciousness writing style of Virginia Woolf.

The diagram illustrates the method by which the letters are constructed. Circular strokes, for example, are drawn, aligned to related strokes, and divided into sections with a knife tool. The small black squares indicate where incisions were made to create the circular stroke of the letter *G*.

The justified columns of text used in the book are well crafted to obtain a consistency of color and space for optimized readability and aesthetic form. When you choose to justify text, the relationship of line length and type size must be critically examined. Two columns set on the same 19-pica measure and in the same typeface (Futura Light) but in dramatically different type sizes differ greatly. The word spacing of the 8-point version appears reasonably consistent (left), while the 12-point version is disrupted with awkward and irregular gaps and valleys between letters and words (right). Generally speaking, as type shrinks in size and line length grows, spacing in the text block appears more consistent and is easier to control.

The hypothesis that there is an ideally correct form for each letter of the alphabet is just as erroneous as Geofroy Tory's simple assumption that there is a relation between the shapes of letters and the human body; erroneous, because the shapes of letters have been in consistent process of modification from their very beginnings. Indeed, the shapes of letters now in daily use are due entirely to a convention, so that in preferring one form to another our only consideration need be for the conventions now existing and the degree in which each satisfies our sense of beauty. It should be kept clearly in mind that "the perfect model of a letter is altogether imaginary and arbitrary. There is a definite model for the human

The hypothesis that there is an ideally correct form for each letter of the alphabet is just as erroneous as Geofroy Tory's simple assumption that there is a relation between the shapes of letters and the human body; erroneous, because the shapes of letters have been in consistent process of modification from their very beginnings. Indeed, the

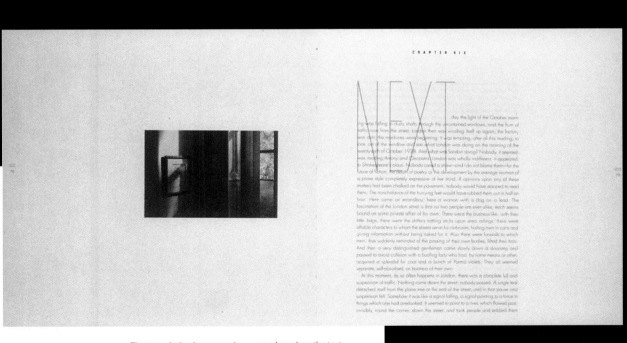

The page design is open and light; the typography restrained yet articulate. The chapter opening above consists of a photograph on the left-hand page that illustrates the romantic scene of the text. The first line of text is indented to accommodate the large word NEXT, which opens the first paragraph and corresponds to the style of type used on the cover. The word overlaps the text, appearing to just skim the surface of the paper. Take note of the typographic refinements: the word's baseline aligns perfectly with the meanline of the ninth line of text, and the middle horizontal stroke of the E aligns with the capline of the first line of text.

Between 1935 and 1943, in the shadow of the Great Depression, artists in America were put to work by the Worker Progress Administration (WPA), and specifically the Federal Art Project. *Posters of the WPA* chronicles this extraordinary period when artists and designers created some of the most important posters of the history of American graphic design. With no creative restrictions placed upon them by the government, they explored new visual terrain and responded to avant-garde thinking that had originated in Europe. The book captures the spirit of these posters in layout, and in the use of typography. Kabel, a typeface designed between 1927 and 1929 by the celebrated German designer, Rudolf Koch, is used exclusively throughout the book. Still in use today, it recalls the typographic sensibilities of the WPA period.

a   b   a

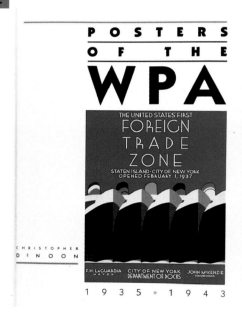

A WPA poster – the central motif of the cover – governs the color, placement, proportions, and spacing of the type and other visual ingredients. Vivid ruled lines separate the title into parts and reveal a graphic persona not unlike the posters of the WPA. The title letters *WPA* are enlarged to give them hierarchical prominence. The title, in concert with the poster image and date line, forms a symmetrical organization.

Whether by plan or by accident, letter combinations can create engaging and eloquent images. The letters *WPA*, for example, linger in the mind's eye because of their shapes and juxtaposition. The letters *W* and *A* share severe, pointed apexes and oblique strokes. The *P*, with a vertical and curved stroke, stands in opposition. At work are the typographic principles of repetition and contrast. The corresponding letters *W* and *A* (a), with their angularity, stand in contrast to the rounded letter *P* (b). The effect is a distinct musical beat (above).

Symmetry and asymmetry are structuring techniques that may be used by typographic designers to organize space. Symmetrical placement produces a quiet, complacent setting, while asymmetry achieves visual tension.

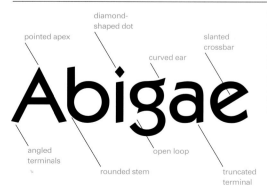

pointed apex

diamond-shaped dot

curved ear

slanted crossbar

angled terminals

rounded stem

open loop

truncated terminal

Despite its continued success as both a text and display typeface, Kabel possesses a few mannerist kinks. Its precise geometry is softened by subtle differences between the thick and thin strokes of letters and a handful of characters with whimsical characteristics.

Under the New Deal, the U.S. Travel Bureau set out to awaken Americans' interest in their homeland. Given the conditions of the time—much of Europe and Asia were embroiled in war in the late 1930s—Americans'

Chapter division pages open with a 2-line drop cap and the first five lines set in 18/24 Kabel Bold. This device energizes the page, makes a declarative statement, and effectively leads the reader into the text (left).

On each page, small black squares are anchored in the outside corners. This repetitive scheme provides visual cohesiveness between the pages. The two top outside squares also function as part of a folio/running head unit, with the folio horizontally positioned and the title of the book vertically positioned. The square, which corresponds in size to the height of the letters, links the two units together (right).

The justified text used throughout the book is set in 12/20 Kabel Medium on a measure of 30.5 picas. New paragraphs are identified with a generous 6-pica indent. The text has no ambition to overpower the showcase of posters, but its formidable typographic color (texture and tone) does reflect the visual vibrance exuding from the posters.

Kabel, like most other type families consists of typefaces of varying weights. The type settings in *Posters of the WPA* takes advantage of these weights and the contrasts they offer. This can be seen in the index, where subjects appear in Kabel Book and numerals referring to illustrations appear in Kabel Bold. Assigning elements different weights helps the reader quickly find the poster he is looking for. The index is set 8/8, line for line (below).

Published by the Library of Congress, *Scrolls from the Dead Sea* chronicles an exhibition of the remarkable scrolls and other artifacts discovered by a Bedouin boy in 1947. The purpose of the catalog is to relate to the public the story of the scrolls' discovery, and to provide a resource for scholars. The design of the catalog, consisting of simple and classical typography, takes into consideration the need to clearly present the texts with their accompanying reproductions, translations, and explanations. Typographic details are carefully addressed, from the choice of typeface and precise text kerning, to the high quality separations of photographs for ensured readability of the texts. It is also significant that the catalog skillfully blends the type of three languages: English, Hebrew, and Greek.

SCROLLS FROM THE DEAD SEA

SCROLLS FROM THE DEAD SEA

The catalog's title is designed to fit into a tight, rectangular shape for an orderly appearance. First decided was how to break the title into distinct lines. It makes good sense that *SCROLLS* stands alone on the first line as the largest and most significant element, for this is the main subject of the catalog. *DEAD SEA* appears on the bottom line at a slightly smaller size, and the lesser words *FROM THE* function as a bridge between the title's top and bottom lines.

To achieve the squarish shape in the title typography, lines of type are optically adjusted to appear vertically aligned on both the right and left sides of the type unit. Optical alignment is not something that can be achieved with a ruler. All letters possess unique shapes, a fact that must be taken into consideration when making any optical adjustment. Compare the optically-aligned letters (right) with the mechanically-aligned letters (far right). Notice how the mechanically-aligned letters actually appear unaligned, as no adjustment has been made to compensate for the differences in letter shape. For example, the curved letter *a* and diagonal letter *v* require lateral shifting in relationship to the *b* to compensate for their unique shapes.

a
b
v

a
b
v

As if emerging from a shadow of the past, a Dead Sea Scroll unfolds across the cover. Mantinia, a typeface with distinctive wedge-shaped serifs, dramatically serves as the title. Interestingly, this type designed by Matthew Carter to function in part as a titling face for Galliard, embodies in design the spirit of ancient Hebrew inscriptions. The flaring strokes, sharp curves, and well-knit texture of the typeface resembles similar qualities in Hebrew characters (below).

The title letters are painstakingly kerned to create tight but comfortable letters pacing and to avoid the nasty spaces often resulting from awkward letter combinations such as between the combinations, *CR, RO,* and *LS.* The ultimate goal in kerning is to strive for the appearance of exactly the same amount of space between letters. Therefore, kerning requirements differ as the overall letter spacing differs. For example, tighter letter spacing requires tighter kerning, while looser letter spacing requires looser kerning. Compare the word *SCROLLS* both kerned (top) and unkerned (bottom).

The catalog's designer, Robert Wiser, not only focuses on the optical spacing issues of display type, he also prepares extensive, custom kerning tables for all of the text faces used in his publications. This ensures a consistency in letter spacing and a readability of the highest order.

AT AV AY
FA LT LV VA
To Vo Ye Sy

Every typeface has a unique set of problems when it comes to kerning, but there are a few basic, notorious character combinations that always need attention. Some of the more obvious and problematic ones are shown to the left.

SCROLLS

SCROLLS

Ancient Hebrew scrolls accidentally discovered in 1947 by a Bedouin boy have kindled popular enthusiasm as well as serious scholarly interest over the past half century. The source of this excitement is what these Dead Sea Scrolls reveal about the history of the Second Temple period (520 B.C.E.–70 C.E.), particularly from the second century B.C.E. until the destruction of the Second Temple in 70 C.E.—a time of crucial developments in the crystallization of the monotheistic religions.

The Judean Desert, a region reputedly barren, defied preconceptions and yielded an unprecedented treasure. The young Ta'amireh shepherd was certainly unaware of destiny when his innocent search for a stray goat led to the fateful discovery of Hebrew scrolls in a long-untouched cave. One discovery led to another, and eleven scroll-yielding caves and a habitation site eventually were uncovered. Since 1947 the site of these discoveries—the Qumran region (the desert plain and the adjoining mountainous ridge) and the Qumran site—have been subjected to countless probes; not a stone has remained unturned in the desert, not an aperture unprobed. The Qumran settlement has been exhaustively excavated.

The first trove found by the Bedouins in the Judean Desert consisted of seven large scrolls from Cave 1. The unusual circumstances of the find, on the eve of Israel's war of independence, obstructed the initial negotiations for the purchase of all the scrolls. Shortly before the establishment of the state of Israel, Professor E. L. Sukenik of the Hebrew University clandestinely acquired three of the scrolls from a Christian Arab antiquities dealer in Bethlehem. The remaining four scrolls reached the hands of Mar Athanasius Yeshua Samuel, Metropolitan of the Syrian Jacobite Monastery of St. Mark in Jerusalem. In 1949 he traveled to the United States with the scrolls, but five years went by before the prelate found a purchaser.

On June 1, 1954, Mar Samuel placed an advertisement in the *Wall Street Journal* offering "The Four Dead Sea Scrolls" for sale. The advertisement was brought to the attention of Yigael Yadin, Professor Sukenik's son, who had just retired as chief of staff of the Israel Defense Forces and had reverted to his primary vocation, archeology. With the aid of intermediaries, the four scrolls were purchased from Mar Samuel for $250,000. Thus, the scrolls that had eluded Yadin's father because of the war were now at his disposal. Part of the purchase price was contributed by D. S. Gottesman, a New York philanthropist. His heirs sponsored construction of the Shrine of the Book in Jerusalem's Israel Museum, in which these unique manuscripts are exhibited to the public.

The seven scrolls from Cave 1, now housed together in the Shrine of the Book, are Isaiah A, Isaiah B, the Habakkuk Commentary, the Thanksgiving Scroll, the Community Rule (or the Manual of Discipline), the War Rule (or the War of Sons of Light Against the Sons of Darkness), and the Genesis Apocryphon, the last being in Aramaic. All the large scrolls have been published.

TREASURES
FROM THE
JUDEAN
DESERT

*Ayala Sussmann
and Ruth Peled*

23

An introduction page shows some of the catalog's representative design attributes. The pages are organized with the aid of a versatile four-column grid. The wide text block displayed here extends across three columns for a total measure of 28 picas.

A two-line drop cap set in Mantinia relates to the cover typography, invites the reader into the page, and punctuates the page with a spot of contrast.

The text is set in 9.9/14.8 Galliard Roman and tracked to 1, which is to add a 1/200-em space between all characters for just a slight amount of letter spacing.

The title of the article, vertically centered on the page and positioned in the last column is set in letter spaced 15.9/23.8 Galliard Roman Small Capitals.

The author's credit is set in 12.9/19.3 Galliard Italic.

An em space introduces new paragraphs.

A justified text setting appears consistent in color and texture, the result of comprehensive kerning, a wide measure and appropriate hyphenation.

Wide margins lend the page an open, dignified appearance.

Nothing fancy about this folio. Positioned in the outside corner of the page, it quietly does its job.

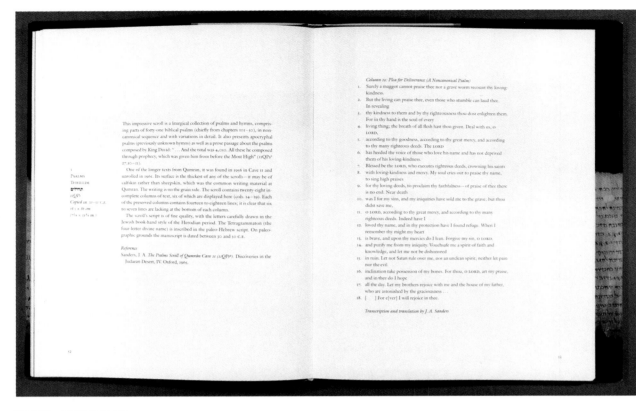

The pages of the book are laid out along a centered, horizontal axis, as seen in the two spreads above. This provides a cohesion between the scrolls of varying shape as well as the blocks of text.

small eye
wedged serif
straight, diagonal stroke
foot serif
heavy serifs
flaired horizontal stroke

Galliard, designed by Matthew Carter in 1978, is an energetic Old-Style font inspired by the 16th century types of punchcutter Robert Granjon. The expressive qualities of the face distinguish it from most other Old-Style types, and it has as a result gained popularity in the areas of book design and advertising. Galliard is crisply drawn with angular features and a good amount of contrast in the strokes of the letters.

Galliard is a family of fonts containing an expansive group of characters, including supplementary characters that greatly expand the possibilities of the typeface. These include a wide range of alternate characters, titling letters, ligatures, Old-Style figures, small capitals, fractions, and other special characters and symbols. These are used to advantage in this book. For example, special fractions are used for the scroll measurements, providing an excellent alternative to manually constructed fractions using superior and inferior figures. It is important to be aware of the full collection of characters in a font. To the right is a detail from the book that effectively utilizes several font options, including Old Style figures, Small capitals, italics, an en-dash, special fractions, brackets, and a special ×️ symbol.

5
PSALMS
TEHILLIM
תהילים
11QPs
Copied ca. 30–50 C.E.
18.5 × 86 cm
(7¼ × 33¾ in.)

כי לוא רמה תודה לכה ולוא תספר חסדכה תולעה .1

חי חי יורה לכה יורו לכה כול מוטטי רגל בהורדיעכה .2

חסדכה להמה וצרקתכה תשכילם כי בירכה נפש כול .3

חי נשמת כול ‎𐤉𐤄𐤅𐤄‎ כשר אתה נתתה עשה עמנו ‎𐤉𐤄𐤅𐤄‎ .4

כטובכה כרוב רחמיכה וכרוב צרקותיכה שמע .5

‎𐤉𐤄𐤅𐤄‎ בקול אוהבי שמו ולוא עזב חסדו מהמה .6

1. Surely a maggot cannot praise thee nor a grave worm recount thy loving-kindness.

2. But the living can praise thee, even those who stumble can laud thee.
   In revealing

3. thy kindness to them and by thy righteousness thou dost enlighten them.
   For in thy hand is the soul of every

4. living thing; the breath of all flesh hast thou given. Deal with us, O LORD,

5. according to thy goodness, according to thy great mercy, and according to
   thy many righteous deeds. The LORD

6. has heeded the voice of those who love his name and has not deprived
   them of his loving-kindness.

Of great interest are the transcriptions of the scroll texts. Because Hebrew characters read from right to left, numerals corresponding to specific lines of text on the scrolls are logically positioned to the right of each line in the transcriptions. Notice also that even the period precedes the numeral rather than following it. The section of scroll transcribed is indicated by a thin bracketed rule line.

Compare the Hebrew transcriptions to the English translations (left). Obviously, the reading direction of the translation is reversed. In keeping with the even line spacing of the scroll text, the spacing of the translation text remains consistent from line to line. A space of eighteen points clearly distinguishes the numerals from the text, and is visually proportional to the line spacing.

Designer:
Robert Wiser

This is a volume about the history, lore, and role of books in human society. It is designed with a reverence for the traditions of book design and typography, and its pages reflect the fine craft associated with the development of the book. Classical in appearance, *The Smithsonian Book of Books* is the embodiment of the principles of book design laid down over the centuries: expressive layout and impeccable typography clothed in fine papers and binding. The text is set in Monotype Bembo, a classic-revival typeface produced in 1929 under the supervision of Stanley Morison. The book's designer, Robert Wiser, created the display typeface, Capitalis. This design of this typeface is patterned after the stone-cut letters on the Trajan Column in Rome.

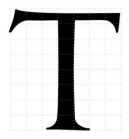

The display type used for the jacket and other titling within the book is the above mentioned Capitalis. Based on the letters inscribed on the Trajan Column, this typeface represents the earliest Roman letters and serves as a meaningful and historical backdrop for the book. Shown here are representative characters from the typeface. The classical proportions of these letters reveal a height that is approximately eight times the stroke width.

Note the similarity in design of Bembo, the book's text face, and Capitalis. The visual affinity of these two typefaces is no accident; each is derived from classical letter-form proportions.

The book's jacket is simple in design with bold colors and visually punchy typography. To avoid overt religious overtones, the title is arranged so that *The Smithsonian Book of* is clearly subordinate to *Books*. This avoids the link of *Book of Books* to the Bible, focusing rather on the greater subject of books. This is an excellent example of how a simple change in emphasis can radically alter meaning. The title is centered over an illuminated initial *S* with King David as a scribe from a 15th-century antiphonary. The color of the title typography relates to the illumination. The jacket's type and image pop out of the black background for a distinctive visual appearance (above).

Appearing on the contents spread with typography are printers' marks from the 15th and 16th centuries. The main chapters are typeset in Bembo Roman capitals with related secondary chapters in Bembo Italic. Though the chapter titles are larger in size than the rest of the type, they are appropriately scaled and not overwhelming. The roomy line spacing between chapters provides a cultivated look, and the groupings of chapters clearly plot the organization of the book for the reader (below).

The grid structure is conventional in nature, consisting of plentiful margins that enclose three columns separated by two picas of space. Where necessary, the grid is violated to achieve a larger image for more impact, or in the case of the chapter divisions to increase the width of the opening column. Sometimes text extends across two columns; on other occasions it occupies single columns. To the credit of the designer, the grid enables astounding variety in the flow and pacing of the pages. Even within the restricted boundaries of a traditional design, one never finds a dull moment (above).

Margins are an extremely important part of a publication's design: they frame elements such as text blocks and illustrations, and they establish the spatial attitude of the publication. Margins may be symmetrically passive or asymmetrically active. No specific rules govern the use of margins, but it is known that unequal margin intervals provide a pleasing visual tension for the page. Violating margins by bleeding elements off the page or placing elements in the margins (marginalia) can be striking. Consider the margin possibilities depicted here.

The two chapter division spreads shown here are representative of the consistent use of full-bleed images on the verso side of the spread and the opening text (discussed on the previous page) on the recto.

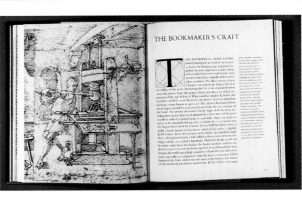

THE GUTENBERG REVOLUTION

IMAGINE THE GREAT FRANK-furt Fair of 1455. There, on a plain trestle table, under a canvas awning, were row after row of Bibles. Some were on vellum, most on paper. There had been more handsome Bibles before, and more sumptuous ones, too. But here the magic was in the calligraphy: perfectly regular, no variance whatsoever. Truly, the scribe who penned this must have sold his soul to the devil. ❡ It must have been a shock. An Italian visitor named Piccolomini recorded that there were very many customers for this new and perfect kind of book, one that was so clear it could be read without spectacles. Its cost? About 30 florins, a clerk's wage for about three years. ❡ The man who made the magical Bibles was a middle-aged businessman named Johann Gensfleisch, who, in the customary way of patrician families in that era, was known by his mother's family name, Gutenberg. From his printing shop in the cathedral town of Mainz, on the Rhine River about 20 miles from Frankfurt, Gutenberg had raised the fledgling "secret arts" of printing to a level of perfection that would never be attained again. He also went broke. ❡ Gutenberg was born in Mainz about 1397, but was forced to flee in his youth because of political troubles. Up the Rhine, in Strasbourg, he began experimenting in metallurgy and in the mass-production of souvenir mirrors for pilgrims to the shrine at Aachen. Gutenberg saw a large market for mirrors and knew that the key to that market was inexpensive production. ❡ But the pilgrimage was not the only path to heaven or riches. There was also the indulgence, a small slip of paper offering sinners

Preceding pages: A 19th-century painting recreates a 15th-century visit by King Edward IV to the printing shop of William Caxton, publisher of the first book printed in English. Opposite, hand-painted illuminations decorate a page from a 15th-century Gutenberg Bible printed on vellum in Mainz, Germany. This copy now resides at the Huntington Library in California. Gutenberg's Bibles were the world's first identically printed books. At left, an initial I from the Biblia Germanica (German Bible), printed in 1483 by Anton Koberger in Nuremberg, Germany.

113

One of the most effective aspects of the book is the chapter divisions which by design are clearly distinguished from other pages. Their visual opulence is the result of several well-planned typographic features.

The recto page opens with an historical illuminated initial. There are different initials for each chapter and each is dropped into a single column of justified, 15/18.2 Bembo Roman.

The first line of text, set in all capitals Bembo, leads the eye into the text block and is a traditional method for opening a chapter or section.

A caption to the right of the text block identifies the initial and a full-bleed image on the facing page.

Paragraphs within the text are indicated by a scribal mark called a pilcrow. Printed in red, these marks add brilliance to the page. The pilcrows are placed within the text with a word space before and after – space that is visually consistent with the rest of the text.

Pilcrows were used by early printers and are still used today by some designers to indicate the beginnings of paragraphs or to serve as reference marks. Many fonts offer a version of this character for a wide variety of choices (left).

Other marks such as fleurons, an elevated term for a dingbat, can be used effectively as paragraph indicators. Select fleurons that are visually compatible with other elements in the design and which relate in some way to the content of the text (left).

Zapf was born in Germany in 1918 and spent much of his youth teaching himself italic letter forms, living laborious days copying the old masters. He was so self-taught, in fact, that it was several years before he discovered he was holding his pen the wrong way. Zapf's early enthusiasm was for modernistic calligraphy, but his ideas changed abruptly when he came across Edward Johnston's *Writing and Illuminating and Lettering* (1906). Reading those pages, Zapf realized that traditional italic letters—faithfully copied and thus deeply understood—would determine his future.

that traditional italic letters—faithfully
that traditional italic letters – faithfully

that traditional italic letters — faithfully
that traditional italic letters–faithfully

Designer:
Matt Woolman

Types (a journey beyond the baseline), written and designed by Matthew Woolman, presents a saga of digital madness in the late twentieth century – a tale of typographic anarchy. The story opens with detectives Fleuron and Dingbat hot on the trail of the outlaws responsible for yet another typographic crime, the mutilation of a letterform beyond recognition. They follow their only clue, a trail of ink splattered across the page. The extensive cast of characters, numbering thirty, includes such classic typefaces as Bembo, Garamond, and Janson, as well as contemporary novelty faces such as Totally Gothic, Variex, and Trixie. The narrator's voice is set in American Typewriter, an appropriate choice for text that reads as a police report. Reading the book increases one's understanding of typographic history and the ability of type to act as both word and image.

k

The cover of the book begins with a portrait of the victim: a lowercase Minion *k*, resting on a baseline (above). The title page cuts to the scene of the crime, with an introduction of a few of the main characters (top right). *Types (a journey beyond the baseline)* entertains and informs the reader with a voyeuristic peek at a typographic world normally hidden from human view, the world of type as image and object. On the next spread, baselines fill the entire page, and as if accompanied by detectives Fleuron and Dingbat, the reader traces the crime by walking through typographic history (bottom right).

Types
[a journey beyond the baseline]

...It all began around 1450,

in Europe, when Johann Gutenberg developed the art of printing with movable metal type on a mechanical press. Gutenberg originally used the letter press for the printing of religious manuscripts, including his forty-two-line Gutenberg Bible in 1455. By the end of the 15th century, at the height of the Italian Renaissance, a scholar and printer named Aldus Manutius set up a press in Venice to print Greek and Roman classics. This initiated a collaboration between Humanists and printers that changed the intellectual life in Europe and the rest of the world. And it is here where the typeface as we know it was born...

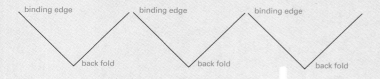

binding edge   binding edge   binding edge

back fold   back fold   back fold

The pages of the book are backfolded, linking pages into a continuous chain of events, much like the frames of a film. Experimenting with bindings can strengthen typographic presentation and enhance content.

Typographic experimentation occurs throughout the book, and the computer is used as a tool to explore the potential of type as picture and to test the limits of legibility. Continuously pasting letter upon letter, for example, generated the crowd of characters congregating in the shadows, as well as the black background for the reversed paragraph (opposite page).

Readability need not be totally disregarded to achieve visual effect. The negative line spacing in the paragraph to the right is not so extreme as to completely destroy readability. However, when characters within lines overlap too much, readability is compromised greatly (bottom right).

the typographic world has fallen into complete digital anarchy. Letterform violence and character assassination has infested the once clean and legible land of the printed word. The culprit or culprits are yet unknown. The only evidence is an ink-spotted trail of broken, stretched and zoomed typographic carnage...

the typographic world has fallen into complete digital anarchy. Letterform violence and character assassination has infested the once clean and legible land of the printed word. The culprit or culprits are yet unknown. The only evidence is an ink-spotted trail of broken, stretched and zoomed typographic carnage...

American Typewriter is an official representative of the ubiquitous family of typefaces highly familiar to those whose fingers (prior to the electronic revolution) clapped along typewriter keyboards. Whereas typewriters mechanically position letters with the same amount of space, computers enable flexible spacing alternatives and unrestricted design possibilities. American Typewriter mechanically spaced (top), and optically spaced with the computer (bottom).

type
type

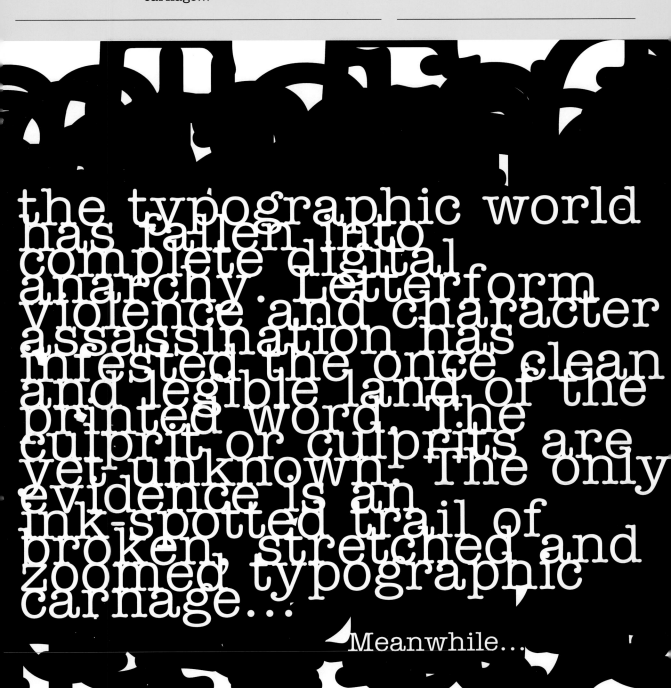

the typographic world has fallen into complete digital anarchy. Letterform violence and character assassination has infested the once clean and legible land of the printed word. The culprit or culprits are yet unknown. The only evidence is an ink-spotted trail of broken, stretched and zoomed typographic carnage...

Meanwhile...

'My name is Detective Fleuron. I am a s veteran in letter violence.

I've seen a lot of letterform crimes in my time but this is b complished without a skew. This form is no longer legible. Notice the severly distorted ascender. All of its serifs have been sever I se ness of the page beyond. Ink is splattered everywhere, revealing a

In the spread above, large letters and quotation marks draw the reader directly and intimately into the verbal dialogue. The scale and overwhelming presence of the forms imply a flurry of investigative activity and an assertive voice; yet, the hidden letterforms and irregular text settings suggest a rather disorganized attempt to solve the mystery and difficulty in getting all of the information surrounding the crime.

The computer is effectively used to reverse the large quotation marks from the black field and to position the partially obstructed type inside them. The quotation marks suggest "windows" through which we may peer to witness the activity. Placing the central quotation mark in a position shared by both pages unifies the spread. When designing pages, visual continuity is preserved by working with spreads in mind.

My partner
is Detective
Dingbat, a
newcomer to
investigative
work.

baseline or grid.
foul play...

Throughout the book, type is
manipulated to suggest
environments, as in this
example where "We trace the
ink spots which lead us
through a forest of question
marks. . ." Here, type is exclusively visual and metaphorical
in nature. Calculatingly
overlapping characters makes
this textural "forest"
possible.

Designers:
Gail Anderson
Lee Bearson
Debra Bishop
Geraldine Hessler
Fred Woodward

Lettering:
Eric Siry

Art Director:
Fred Woodward

The designers of *Rolling Stone,* a popular rock and roll magazine that originated in the early 1970s, creatively employ the computer for expressive and interpretive typography and images. The computer is not merely used as a production tool; it is ambitiously approached as a resource for creative inspiration and form exploration. The magazine, utilizing a staggering array of classical as well as recent typefaces, provides an excellent source for the study of contemporary type usage. Each cover and article opening reponds typographically and pictorially to upbeat and vivid content, transporting the reader into the sensuous and resonant domain of popular culture and music. In this sense, the magazine's typography not only records information; it also illuminates, enhances, and extends the content.

Mixing typefaces can be a tricky business, and the best results come from combining fonts that bear no resemblance to one another. Excellent examples of this principle are found in the two *Rolling Stone* covers shown here. Woody Condensed is combined with Bodoni in a cover featuring a highly sensuous photograph of Janet Jackson. With the aid of the computer, a soft cast shadow has been added to the type, pulling it forward in space. The visual dynamics of the cover is further enhanced with a photo of Janet Jackson overlapping the *Rolling Stone* masthead (left).

The second example (below) is a cover that dangerously but effectively combines five different fonts. Overlapping a color portrait of the rock group R.E.M. are two sans serif typefaces, Saracen and Woody Block Condensed. The titles are hand-lettered with the computer to appear as three-dimensional letters in perspective. Combining two similar sans serif typefaces normally leads to disastrous results. But the varied width, color, and perspective of this union offers sufficient, even lively contrast. Other fonts used on the cover are Leviathan, Ziggurat, and Acropolis Italic, designed by Jonathan Hoefler.

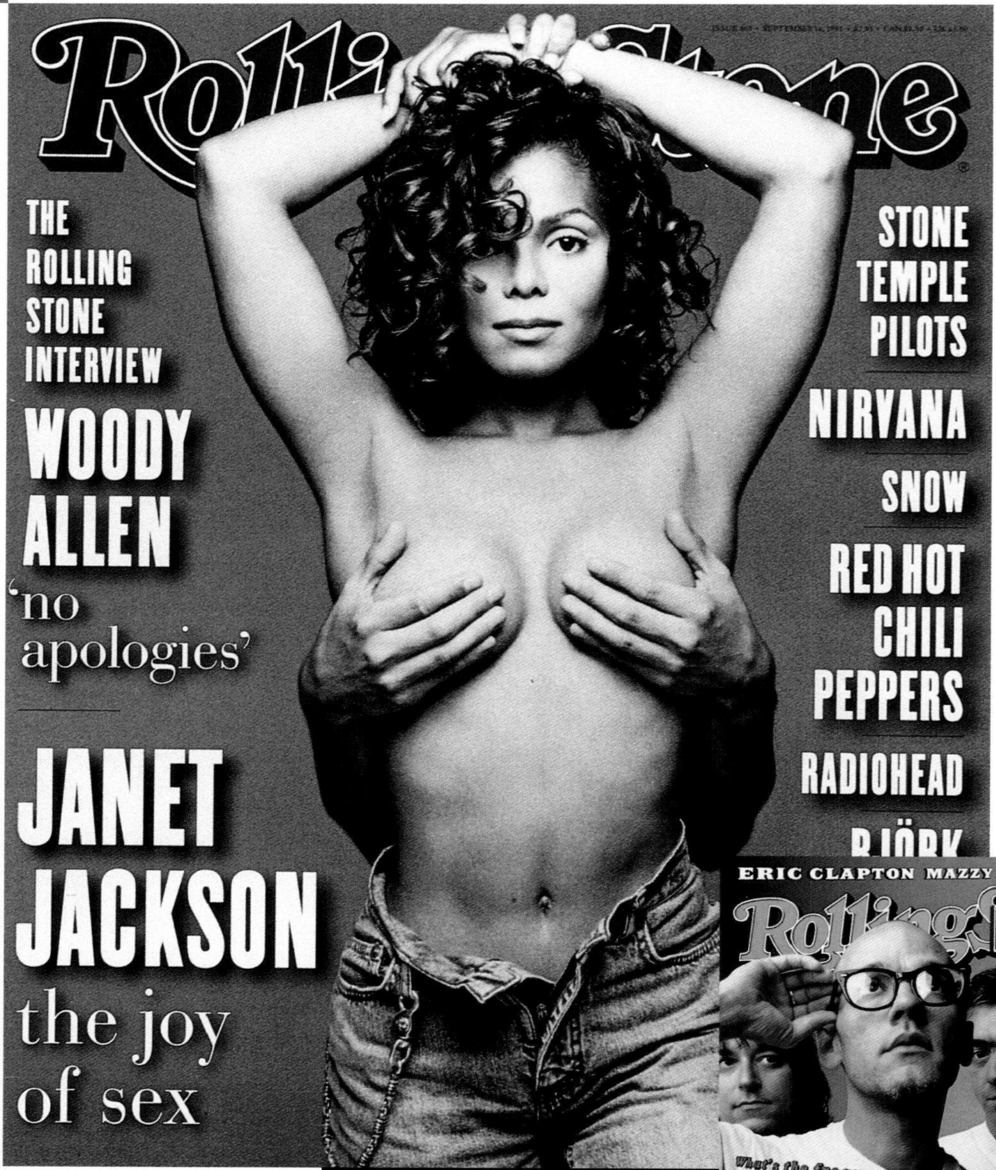

Drawing programs enable you to create shadows for type, and the degree of hardness or softness for a shadow can readily be controlled. One must experiment with the many ways of creating shadows to achieve the desired effect.

The word *LETTERMAN* is typeset in Empire, a highly condensed typeface. Stretched even further with the computer, the dramatically vertical letters reach from the top of the page to the bottom, creating an eccentric and off-beat title for an interview with David Letterman. *David* is set in Kuenstler Script for contrast (right).

An intensely nervous pattern of letters is achieved by overlapping and squashing letters together, and assigning different colors to individual letters and counterforms. The typeface is Champion Gothic by Jonathan Hoefler (below).

The title *Zoo World Order* is typeset in horizontally stretched and overlapping Egyptienne letters. The intersecting spaces created by the overlapping letters appear as white, giving the words a reflective, transparent quality (right).

xxxLifeAfterDeath xxx
xxxx
Courtneyl0ve
xxphotographxx
by Mark Seliger xxx

David

Trixie, a typeface remniscent of typewriter characters but more expressive and informal in quality, is used for *Life After Death: The Rolling Stone Interview with Courtney Love.* This typeface is an appropriate choice for an interview consisting of frank but honest questions and answers about life and death. In the title, characters bump into one another and bounce up and down. The typographic symbol for love, *xxxx*, found in the title is a reference for both Courtney Love's name and the human emotion of love.

For an article entitled *Monster Madness,* Gill Sans letters are extruded, rendered as colorful, three-dimensional forms and positioned on an ellipse to form a halo. This effectively encircles the bald head pictured in a black and white portrait photograph.

MONSTER MADNESS

MICHAEL STIPE

38 · ROLLING STONE, OCTOBER 20, 1994

The letters *S, M,* and *H* are rendered with a perspective tool to appear as though they are floating in space.

Overlapping letters transform two-dimensional planes into active three-dimensional environments. The degree of overlap, typeface, color, tone, scale, and specific arrangement of elements enable many different effects.

depth depth depth depth depth

PETER BUCK

Grecian, a bold, slab-serif font with characteristically angled corners is used for the title of this article about James Hetfield of the rock group Metallica. The letters, set at different sizes and colors, and overlapping one another, form a screaming, kinetic, and dimensional pattern.

Champion letters are skewed and combined with a wire-frame drawing of the letters for a kinetic, three-dimensional effect. The text type, set in Cloister and also skewed, conforms to the front plane of a cube-like structure.

SLIPPIN' AROUND ON THE ROAD WITH BRAD

BEHOLD BRAD PITT. Everyone else seems to be. On the way to this particular London pub, no less than three young ladies have come skulking out of the shadows to solicit a favor from said heartthrob. Each case is the same: A woman approaches demurely, flashes a

smile in desperate need of quality dentistry and utters the question "Excuse me, are you Brad Pitt?" The answer quite obviously being yes, the script continues: "Do you think I could get a

Type pictorially suggests a highway system for an article entitled *Slippin' Around on the Road with Brad Pitt.* To create this typographic metaphor, the stems of Champion Gothic letters in the word *PITT* are lengthened and printed in black. For a convincing simulation of highway dividing line, the author's credit is set in yellow, stacked letters that run down the center of the *I*. Colorful letters forming *BRAD* are woven into *PITT*, providing a unified and rhythmic composition. The precise alignments of the overlapping vertical and horizontal letters suggest intersections of roads.

Roman Compressed type expresses in a title that the Rolling Stones are taking their "rock and roll circus" back on the road. Calculated scale shifts and deliberate positioning of the letters enable the dot of the *i* to read as a human eye, and the lower-case *e* in the word *Time* to double as a dot for the exclamation mark.

Bell Centennial is a rather gloomy typeface with exaggerated features such as flaring strokes and sharp counters. But there is also something elegant about the design, its curves suggesting the marks inscribed upon ice by figure skaters. This typeface is an excellent choice for an article entitled *Tanya Harding: The Hard Fall*. The *HARD* in *HARDING* is printed in black and gray ink to obtain a double reading, and the ruled lines separating different parts of the title further suggest tracks left on the ice by skaters.

A pageant of color and interlocking shapes celebrate an article entitled *Man of the Year: David Letterman*. The similarities between the illustration and the title typography provide visual cohesiveness. The typeface used is Smokler.

Designer:
Frank Armstrong

The Bridgeport Hospital *Resource Magazine* is published to inform the community of changes and developments in the hospital's healthcare programs. The issue shown here announces the merging of two hospitals into a single institution. The headline on the cover, "Weaving a Stronger Network of Care," editorially reflects this merger, and throughout the publication, letters and lines of type are visually woven together as a metaphor for fabric. Two sans serif typefaces, Frutiger Black and Univers Ultra Thin, are combined with a serif typeface, Meridien, for a compatible union.

The Fabric of

By inserting Univers Ultra Thin letters into the counter-spaces of Frutiger Ultra Black letters, a "woven" effect related to the theme of the magazine is achieved.

A two-column grid manages the design and typographic arrangement of this 6"x 11" publication. The columns are 14 picas wide, providing an effective line length for the primary text type, 9/12 Meridien Medium. Two picas separate the columns. The text is set flush-left, ragged right, and an additional 4 points of space separate the paragraphs.

Emerging in a subtle manner from the background of the cover, which is a pattern of gauze, is a photograph of a nurse helping an elderly patient. The reader is immediately introduced to the contents of the magazine with the headline "Weaving a Stronger Network of Care." The reader first reads the word *Weaving*, emphasized in white and introducing the magazine's theme. The rest of the title is then read to complete the message. This appears in the same hue as the background and photo but is darker in value.

RMEASGOAUZRICNEE

By 1992, "the future of Park City Hospital as a stand-alone entity was bleak," says **James G. Woods,** former chairman of Park City's Board of

By 1992, "the future of Park City Hospital as a stand-alone entity was bleak," says James G. Woods, former chairman of Park City's Board of

By 1992, "the future of Park City Hospital as a stand-alone entity was bleak," says James G. Woods, former chairman of Park City's Board of

By 1992, "the future of Park City Hospital as a stand-alone entity was bleak," says JAMES G. WOODS, former chairman of Park City's Board of

By 1992, "the future of Park City Hospital as a stand-alone entity was bleak," says *James G. Woods*, former chairman of Park City's Board of

By 1992, "the future of Park City Hospital as a stand-alone entity was bleak," says **James G. Woods,** former chairman of Park City's Board of

"As technology is saving more lives

and the population is aging, there

is more need for rehabilitation to

Sally Gammon,

help people get back to a full,

president,

productive life."

Rehabilitation

Center of Fairfield

County

"As technology is saving more lives and the population is aging, there is more need for rehabilitation to

"As technology is saving more lives and the population is aging, there is more need for rehabilitation to

Over the past few issues of *Resource* we have focused on a number of factors that are important when it comes to your healthcare, from community services to quality management to research and education. None of these issues is more timely than the one we feature in this issue: the recent merger of Park City Hospital with Bridgeport Hospital.

Designer:
Roger E. Baer

The *Journal of the Design Communication Association* is designed to create a scholarly appearance and to preserve the integrity of the writings of each contributor. Two typefaces are used throughout the publication: Garamond, which provides a scholarly, readable text; and Univers, which stands as a counterpoint to the older Garamond and provides a broad palette of variations for use in heads, subheads, and emphasized elements within the text. Unlike a majority of journals, this one balances plentiful text with a variety of images and a skillful use of white space. Other design tactics, such as a unique system of icons used to identify the pages associated with specific articles, help the reader to navigate the journal's contents.

Scholarly journal

A highly pictorial cover juxtaposes loosely drawn sketches and diagrams with rectangular photographs. The title, *Representation,* is set in Univers 65. Appearing as widely spaced capital letters, it expresses the formality and serious intent of the journal. Even though the title is not visually distinguished from the images in size or in color, it is readily discernable to the reader.

Word recognition is partly based on the shape of words. Words set in all capital letters have the same rectangular shape, whereas words set in lower-case letters have different shapes depending on the specific composition of letters. One reason text type set in all capitals is more difficult to read than text set in capitals and lower-case is because of the lack of variation in word shape. For display titles such as in this journal, however, the use of all capitals is appropriate.

REPRESENTATION

representation

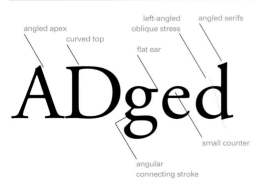

angled apex
curved top
left-angled
oblique stress
angled serifs
flat ear

ADged

small counter
angular
connecting stroke

Garamond is an Old-Style typeface based on the 16th-century types of Claude Garamond. Many versions are now available, each one with distinctly different design characteristics. The version used in the journal and shown here is Adobe Garamond designed by Robert Slimbach. Garamond is one of the most popular typefaces of this century and will undoubtedly remain a favorite into the next century.

A three-column grid is the organizational basis of this journal. A narrow column for heads, running heads, captions, and images rests on the outside of each page; two wider columns reserved for the main text and images appear on the inside of each page. The running text is set flush left, ragged right and is sized and spaced for optimum readability. The journal as a whole is clean and spacious, with strong contrasts between typographic components and images.

Conventional notes revealing sources are listed at the ends of journal articles. Compare a sample note from the journal (top right) to a less desirable facsimile (bottom right). Two things are wrong with the bottom example. First, the quotation marks were made by mistakenly using the double prime, which is an abbreviation for inches. This is not to be confused with the designated quotation marks of the type font. Secondly, the italics were generated by "selecting italics" under the computer's style menu. This does not provide true italics, but a sloped version of roman letters. Always use an italic that is a member of a specific type family.

4. William R. Benedict, "Parti: New Paint for an Old Lady," M. Hardy and T. McGinty. ed., *Proceedings of the 8th Annual Beginning Student Conference*, (Tempe, Arizona: College of Architecture and Environmental Design, Arizona State University, 1991): 17-19.

4. William R. Benedict, "Parti: New Paint for an Old Lady," M. Hardy and T. McGinty. ed., *Proceedings of the 8th Annual Beginning Student Conference*, (Tempe, Arizona: College of Architecture and Environmental Design, Arizona State University, 1991): 17-19.

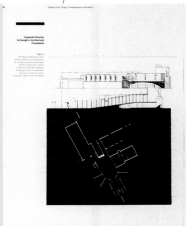
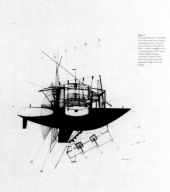

On the verso pages, captions in the ouside column are set flush right, ragged left. On the recto pages they are are set flush left, ragged right. Setting the captions in this mirrored manner lends symmetry and variety to the spreads. Explore in your own publications the controlled use of different text alignments.

The typography in this journal has one purpose only: to present as objectively as possible the scholarly articles. Subsequently, it is not boastful in its visual appearance; rather, it tries only to be a humble but dignified carrier of the content. In the spread above, the small captions dutifully and unobtrusively identify the illustrations.

The hypothesis that there is an ideally correct form for each letter of the alphabet is just as erroneous as Geofroy Tory's simple assumption that there is a relation between the shapes of letters and the human body; erroneous, because the shapes of letters have been in consis-

The hypothesis that there is an ideally correct form for each letter of the alphabet is just as erroneous as Geofroy Tory's simple assumption that there is a relation between the shapes of letters and the human body; erroneous, because the shapes of letters have been in consis-

Setting text flush left, ragged right is more the norm than setting text flush right, ragged left. When optimum readability is desired, the second method, which is disturbing to the reader, should only be used for small amounts of copy such as captions. On the left, compare examples of both methods of text alignment.

Two pages challenge our notion about what is imagined and what is real. Nan Norvell, in Time, Space and "Millions," casts transformation in a new light and graphically examines the issues of process

Two pages challenge our notion about what is imagined and what is real. Nan Norvell, in "Time, Space and Millions," casts transformation in a new light and graphically examines the issues of process and reality that can be manipulated by context and

Two pages challenge our notion about what is imagined and what is real. Nan Norvell, in "Time, Space and Millions," casts transformation in a new light and graphically examines the issues of process and reality that can be manipulated by context and technology, as

The journal's text is set on a 16-pica measure in 10/12 Garamond with normal tracking. These specifications provide excellent spacing and readability. When lines are set shorter or longer, however, an adjustment in tracking and line spacing is required. Shorter lines generally call for tighter tracking and less interline spacing. Longer lines need looser tracking and more space between lines. Above, three text blocks reflect these adjustments.

The notion that opposites attract is true not only of people, but of typefaces as well. Every typeface possesses a unique physical appearance and personality, and when unrelated typefaces are united by plan or by accident, surprising results come about. Ronn Campisi, the designer of *Regional Review,* is a typographic matchmaker well-known for his ability to engineer dangerous liaisons from the most unlikely typeface combinations. The series of magazine covers featured below reflects Campisi's ingenuity and exposes his long-term love affair with type. The computer offers a tool to speedily and spontaneously explore unusual typeface combinations, but such exploration is only useful insofar as the type treatments reinforce or enhance the content of the message.

In the title, *The Bytes of Information,* italic letters mix well with roman, and condensed and extended letters form an agreeable union. The arrangement of the title elements further unifies these varied typefaces.

Covers for *Regional Review* are finely crafted from creative concepts. The typefaces and their visual manipulations are chosen for their ability to communicate. For example, the tall initial *H,* typeset in Bauer, alludes through scale and position to a high-rise building, relating to the title *How Much is that Building in the Window?* What makes this design visually successful is a lively mix of letterform qualities: tall/wide, large/small, capitals/lowercase, and tight/loose spacing. The mixture of color and black and white, and the studied arrangement of the parts also come into play.

Bern is an extremely condensed typeface that reflects the content of the title, *The Thin Red Line (left).* Stacking the words on top of one another and juxtaposing them with the visually organic illustration exaggerates their thinness.

Designs for magazines and other periodicals often evolve over time. This cover introduces a change in the design of the masthead. A new typeface, tighter letter spacing, and a reduction in the size of the letters *O* and *E* improve and refine the cover. Take a look at these changes in the covers presented on these pages.

A key to combining different display typefaces is to accumulate a wide range of specimens for selection and comparison. It is important to keep up with the latest typeface releases by getting on manufacturer's mailing lists and collecting current type specimen books. But access to these resources is only a beginning. Conducting a typeface orchestra requires a sensitive command of all parts. Done well, combining different display types leads to visual bravura and enhanced communication; done poorly, it butchers the page into a cacophonic mess.

To the right are a few basic recipes for the successful mixture of display types. A recipe alone, however, does not ensure a successful gourmet meal. Typographic composition requires practice, skill, and experience.

thin/thick

small/large

italic/roman

script/roman

light/dark

condensed/extended

serif/sans serif

angled/upright

In this *Regional Review* cover, a troupe of letterforms mingles in an effort to reflect the content of the magazine's feature article. The title word *STATE* is set in Latin Wide, a dignified typeface with wedge-shaped serifs reminiscent of nineteenth-century wood types. This typeface contradicts the floral-like qualities of Schulschrift, the typeface used for the word *of* and the capital *N* in *Nature.* Notice the visual similarities of Schulschrift and the delicate bouquet of flowers in the illustration.

Federal Reserve Bank of Boston

REGIONAL REVIEW

STATE

of

Nature

Environmental policy has been driven too much by impulse, too little by reason. Let's direct our resources toward the serious risks and forego the trivial.

Designers:
Brett M. Critchlow
Scott Patt

Art director:
Lanny Sommese

Typography is governed by the visual dynamics of contrast and tension: black and white, light and dark, thick and thin, large and small. The qualities arising from these attributes challenge the eye, provide resonance, guide the reader through the information, and invite active participation in the communication process. While remaining readable, this journal of art criticism, printed entirely in black and white, explores the boundaries of typographic contrast, questions tradition, and tests accepted theories of legibility. The computer provided the designers with a tool that enabled them to deviate from predictable visual outcomes. The wide selection of typefaces used, and their integration into the pages, parallels the literary tension found in the journal's critical essays.

THE PENN STATE
JOURNAL
OF CONTEMPORARY
CRITICISM

five

On the cover set in Helvetica Ultra Compressed, the cropped numeral *5*, which identifies the number of the issue, invites the reader to mentally complete its shape. The numeral disappears behind a white curtain of space. Rules of contrasting lengths and widths appear as appendages to the numeral, abstracting the form and creating a vivid image. The visual luminance of the cover is a result of these varied forms, the stark contrast between the black ink and white paper, and the abundance of white space.

An important goal for any publication is to create visually unified pages. This is partly accomplished in this journal by presenting information in the same way from page to page. For example, on the contents page a large, cropped lower-case *c* is presented in the same way that the numeral *5* appears on the cover.

The journal is filled with visually dynamic type configurations such as the content listings on the contents page, which are set at a 90°angle to mimic the verticality of the large lower-case *c*.

To avoid any confusion for the reader, the word *five* also appears on the cover to help in the mental completion of the cropped numeral *5*. The word overlaps the numeral with letters in both black and white. As a general rule, extremely condensed typefaces are more difficult to read than those of normal width, and those with heavy stroke weights are even more difficult to read. This is due to the diminishing size of the counters. Use should depend on factors such as the amount of copy, size of type, and type style. Compare the readability of the top three words set in different weights of Helvetica Compressed to the same word set in Neue Helvetica 65, a medium-weight typeface of normal width.

five

five

five

five

This large numeral has a striking appearance on the page. Using letters at a large scale has a profound impact on the space, particularly when juxtaposed with smaller elements. Most often, type in books is scaled to a relatively small size and grandiose letters are rarely seen. If you wish to make an impact with type, consider (when appropriate) enlarging them to monumental proportions. For the reader, viewing enormous letters on an ordinary page is like standing next to the Washington Monument. The ruled line running vertically through the large *5* indicates where the numeral is cropped on the cover.

ROBERT MORRIS:
THE LABYRINTH
AND THE HUNTER

Beyond the meticulously constructed facades of Robert Morris's early Minimal works, within the identities of the cast pieces, and beneath the detached demeanor of the artist as performer were meanings virtually impenetrable to viewers in the sixties. But like *Voice* of 1974, with its subliminal soundtracks which dramatize the blunt definition of space by sound into a psychodrama of shattering import. Morris's works of the sixties and seventies were fraught with a tension that belies the apparent matter-of-factness of their structures. Morris's art is generally regarded as having changed abruptly from decade to decade. Yet his focus on the unspeakable carnage and devastation of twentieth century warfare in the drawings/ installations and reliefs of the eighties exposes themes embedded in the cool surfaces that preceded them. The labyrinth and the hunter are introduced in installations and performances of the early sixties, and over the years emerge as images of the human condition.

Opening one of the doors in Morris's loft in 1961, the visitor entered directly into a passageway

8-foot high and the width of the doorway, this seemed initially a plausible corridor. Gradually though it narrowed, its walls describing the converging circumferences of two slightly offset circles. The enveloping gray corridor began to close in; the visitor reached a dead end some 50 feet along and turned back. *Passageway* required the physical involvement of the viewer/ participant; it introduced an imagery of false starts and dead ends, of space under duress.

In *Arizona*, performed at the Judson Memorial Church in 1963, the artist's virtually imperceptible movement was at odds with the frenzied scene conjured by a tape-recorded text explaining "A method for sorting cows." Bare feet planted on the stage, Morris turned his torso 90 degrees in the course of five minutes, while his disembodied voice set forth the method. "It is essential to have a long corridor or alley with a large room or pen off to one side....There are a head man and a gate man. The head man, positioned in the midst of the cows, commands their

attention "by suddenly raising both arms, straight out, bending both knees slightly into a kind of ply, dropping the upper part of his body and at the same time bumping with the lower." The gate man sets his feet well apart, ready for action, gripping his gate. The head man maneuvers to the right, the cows inching toward the left where the gate is.

And so it goes.

until one cow will bolt out and down the left side of the corridor past the head man. But this is exactly what the head man wants. He knows just what to do with this cow: as it bolts he screams "by" or "in". If it is the former the gate man flattens himself against the gate and attempts to become part the wall: if it is the latter, he immediately springs out into the corridor pulling the gate open. The cow will dart into the pen and he slams the gate and freezes to immobility and intense concentration on the head man....

Presumably the curious ritual laid out in the text revolves around life and death choices. But the motive for this odd dance is never stated, only imagined. And the leaping and gesticulating is described against the artist's near immobility. This strange drama of the text concludes with the final cow trotting rather than bolting down the corridor

to "its destined in or by place." "The head man must then turn to his gate man and say, "That's the one we're looking for."

In the second part of *Arizona*, Morris threw a javelin at a target, overlaying the Johnsian imagery of targets with a specter of primitive hunting. Swinging two blue lights he lassoes in the third part, Morris extended the space of the work physically and psychologically into the realm of the spectators. The house lights faded to darkness, while the circle demarked by the blue lights grew progressively bigger. In the fourth and final section, Morris worked with a T-square, a device of delineation and representation.

The choreography of spare and repetitious action seemed perhaps in 1963 an investigation of Minimal sequence. And the javelin throwing might have read as a Duchampian exposé of Johns's investigation of cubist space, with its contradictory play of flatness and depth. But the subtext of *Arizona* was hunting.

We descendents of Cromagnan man...look back with self-congratulation to what we call the first great art on earth - the Magdalenian cave painting of 17,000 years ago...It was a time when game had become less plentiful and humans

---

mary jean
kenton's
freedom
(with limits)

The interpretation of art often implicitly relies on illusions of closure which conceal the complexity, ambiguity, and exercises of power in any era, encouraging audiences to project the generalized motives of an approach or movement onto any artist whose work resembles that style. This issue is relevant to Mary Jean Kenton's art which has a variety of sources rather than one distinct allegiance and does not fall into a single category. Kenton is an artist and writer whose artwork of the last twenty years consists of painted systemic abstractions and related installations. She has long

---

Letterforms in the top example meander in and around text columns to create a typographic labyrinth reflective of the title. The bottom spread, active with types of different sizes and weights, animates the space. The word *freedom* extends across the entire spread, demanding visual attention.

In typography, repetition plays a significant role. The word *freedom* is memorable due to a repetition of the rounded letters *eedo*. The use of the typeface Insignia, consisting of perfectly round characters, and the slight overlap of these characters emphasizes the repetition. When working with display type, look for word patterns such as this to create visual interest.

The paragraph opening shown below provides a very strong but irregular texture due to the condensed Industria letterforms and negative line spacing (-4.2 points). Here, readability is compromised, but perhaps this out-of-control setting is warranted since its visual character relates to the content of the article, art created by schizophrenic people. Also, since this treatment is minimally confined to the opening sentence of each paragraph, the reader is not overly taxed with difficult reading. After the first sentence, the text assumes a more normative appearance with appropriate sizing and line spacing.

The art of the Prinzhorn Collection has held altering positions of privilege and neglect throughout the century, as have the schizophrenic people who helped produce it. The 1922 publication of Hans Prinzhorn's book, The *Artistry of the Mentally Ill*, signalled the peak of the "first wave" of an intense popular fascination with the insane which had been growing steadily since the early 1800's. Romanticism set the tone in

Had the designer desired a more normative setting for the paragraph openings, which of course is not the case, an excellent option would have been to provide more space between the lines and to establish a flush-left, ragged-right alignment. The implementation of these two options are shown here.

Compare this setting with the actual text shown in the above example. Any time you wish to create special computer effects, make sure you have a good reason to do so. Otherwise, the tool is more of a hindrance than a benefit to communication.

The art of the Prinzhorn Collection has held altering positions of privilege and neglect throughout the century, as have the schizophrenic people who helped produce it.

another
other
feminism
and the
prinzhorn
collection

o e d

The grid for this article is composed of two widely-spaced columns per page, with generous margins on all sides. The article title is precisely organized to fit within the left column, thus aligning with the text in the right column. This gives the page a very orderly appearance, which contrasts with some of the more gymnastic type treatments.

This compelling title accentuates the article with tight letter and line spacing and vertical letter strokes that join from line to line. Two vertical rules (indicated above in red) link all of the lines into a unified group. Often, the specific physical features of typefaces lend opportunities for visual enhancements such as this.

Letters are the expression of both form (the strokes of letters) and counterform (the spaces within and around letters). Together these parts determine the visual personalities of letters. Industria is a rather mechanical-looking typeface because of its rectangular counters.

Designers:
Detlef Fiedler
Daniela Haufe

Form + Zweck (Form + Purpose) is a magazine for design, with articles running the gamut of contemporary design criticism and analysis. To enter its pages is to become immersed in a dialogue between architectonic typography and haunting, sensuous photography. The mesmerizing text is set in Bureau Grotesque. Dense, scholarly, and impeccably engineered, it is remniscent of fractur (also known as *black letter*), a traditional form of typography used in Germany beginning in the 16th century. Often giving the impression of being imprisoned behind the text, photographic imagery in a melancholic mix of historical, dance, and theatrical subjects appears to have a life of its own beyond the text.

The credits/contents spread vibrates with kinetic activity. The credits are set into dense, interlocking, and neatly manicured text blocks. Some are set vertically, others horizontally (left).

A detail of the credits page shows how key elements are emphasized through color and the use of all capital letters. This technique makes the information easier to find, and creates a spattered visual pattern (above).

This spread is indicative of the ingenious blending of text and image. On the left page, a figure dances behind a screen of two text columns. The text contains no spatial pauses; new paragraphs are indicated by printing the first two or three words in a second color. End-of-article credits are positioned vertically to square up and complete the rectangular configuration (below).

For the contents page, a photograph sliced into horizontal strips forms a cinematic image. Text announcing the content is tucked tightly between the strips (see spread above and detail below).

Article division spreads consist of large, full-bleed photomontages. Black bars containing article titles stretch across the spread. These move systematically **downward from the beginning of the division spreads to the end.**

This detail demonstrates the maze-like interrelatedness of text and image. Blue lines reveal the alignments establishing order among parts. Take note that no detail is left unattended. The computer enables absolute precision and craft.

While text is always arranged in the basic two-column format, varied expressions of the two columns lend mystery and intrigue from page to page. Here, the two columns suggest continents that were once joined, but which over time have migrated apart. Tucked behind the text blocks are enigmatic photographic fragments. The space separating the two text blocks forms a distinct negative shape.

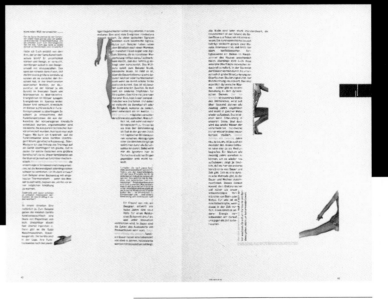

A detail from the spread on the opposite page shows the typographic treatment of article end notes. Numerals identifying the notes are embedded within a rectangular block and printed in black; the notes themselves are printed in yellow-orange. An upside-down grouping of dancers adds a whimsical flavor to the page. The black rectangle to the right of the notes contains a running head and is found on each recto page of the magazine. This rectangle corresponds to the black bars on the division spreads described above (below).

The blackness or visual density of text can be altered by choice of typeface and the amount of space introduced between lines. Compare the density of the two text blocks below. These are set in Univers Ultra Condensed, a typeface with "heavy" characteristics. Adding space between lines gives the text a lighter appearance, in spite of the heaviness of the typeface.

The hypothesis that there is an ideally correct form for each letter of the alphabet is just as erroneous as Geofroy Tory's simple assumption that there is a relation between the shapes of letters and the human body; erroneous, because the shapes of letters have been in consistent process of modification from their very beginnings. Indeed, the shapes of letters now in daily use are due entirely to a

The hypothesis that there is an ideally correct form for each letter of the alphabet is just as erroneous as Geofroy Tory's simple assumption that there is a relation between the shapes of letters and the human body; erroneous, because the shapes of letters have been in consistent process of modification from their very

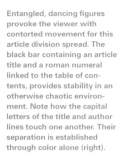

Entangled, dancing figures provoke the viewer with contorted movement for this article division spread. The black bar containing an article title and a roman numeral linked to the table of contents, provides stability in an otherwise chaotic environment. Note how the capital letters of the title and author lines touch one another. Their separation is established through color alone (right).

DIE ZUKUNFT AUF SILIZIUMBASIS
FRIEDRICH KITTLER

Three representative spreads show the visual variety achieved in the publication's text. In an article featuring a discussion between three people, a different color of text is assigned to each. As a counterpoint to the horizontal text, the identifying names of discussion participants are set in small type, positioned vertically, and tucked into the main text blocks (above). In a spread from the same article, a procession of figures photographed by Edward Muybridge flows across the spread. The scale of these figures provides the text with a monumental, architectural quality (right). In yet another section of the magazine, the computer is used to trans-

IV

Designers:
Andrew Henderson
Jan Jancourt

The *Utne Reader* is an alternative magazine devoted to publishing articles that encourage readers to act upon and participate in the ideas and issues they are concerned about. The magazine is serious in tone, thoughtful, and provocative, and a new design for the magazine reflects these qualities. The layout is consistent, clean and uninterrupted by needless embellishment; the crisp typography is geared to objectively and deliberately guide the reader through the content. Where type does open its boundaries to expression and emotion, it judiciously occurs on the opening pages of major articles where titles and subtitles respond to the diverse content. The *Utne Reader* strikes an appropriate balance between type that is easily read and type that is actively and pleasurably viewed.

The redesign of the *Utne Reader* was introduced with this dynamic cover. Several new design features appear, including a masthead with the name of the magazine set in bold capital letters, and teasers of the book's contents separated with bullets. The masthead also features the debut of Officina, the typeface used throughout the publication for titling, running heads, and text type where appropriate. Thin ruled lines divide the cover into zones (masthead, date, slogan, price, and main cover) and are used consistently within the magazine as an organizational technique. The title takes effective advantage of the computer's ability to layer words and images for visual impact.

Notice Officina's unique design characteristics: the oblique terminals, angled stems of letters such as the *b* and *p*, the curved stroke of the *l*, and the square shape of the *i* and *j*.

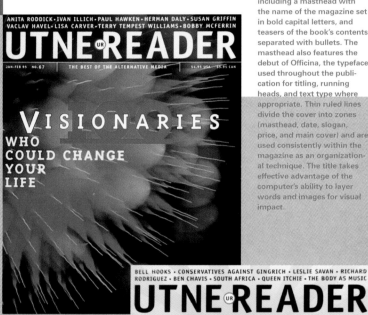

In terms of photography, color, and the typographic treatment of the title, this cover looks very different from that above. However, the use of a consistent masthead, typeface, and ruled lines provide unity. The black shadows placed behind the red letters make the type sit up in the space.

The magazine's two primary typefaces, Times New Roman and Officina, make a good team. Times Roman flavors the publication with tradition; Officina gives it a contemporary feel.

This sample contents page demonstrates the unique use of ruled lines and colored boxes to highlight key information, such as stories and the page numbers where they can be found. Compare the detail below with the method used on the cover to zone information. This is a system that visually unifies the publication and makes information easy to find.

A flexible grid allows the optional use of two and three columns. Sometimes, to achieve variety, they are used simultaneously. Text columns are set justified in Times New Roman. The size of the type is 9-point when it appears in the narrow columns, and 10-point when it appears in the wide columns. This adjustment affords optimum readability for both the two- and three-column settings. Here, the use of a color tint distinguishes two separate but related parts of an article. Also, this spread reveals the use of centered heads – set in all-capitals Officina – within articles.

Adding to the drama and visual electricity of the magazine is the use in article openings of large, evocative photographs. These fill entire pages and are integrated with expressive titles. The text appearing in article openings takes advantage of the two-column grid option, and often sports a drop cap that establishes a clear entry point for the reader.

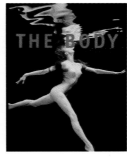

Times New Roman, designed in 1932 by the English typographer and type historian Stanley Morison, is by far the most popular text face in desktop publishing. Highly readable, it is an Old Style typeface exhibiting excellent proportions, and a family consisting of numerous weights and widths.

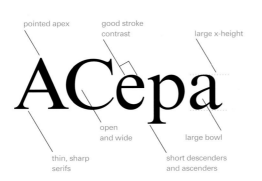

pointed apex

good stroke contrast

large x-height

open and wide

large bowl

thin, sharp serifs

short descenders and ascenders

ACepa

Designer:
Mirko Ilić

Typically, magazines use photographs or illustrations combined with typographic headlines to introduce lead stories on their covers. But letterforms alone have the ability to communicate as illustration, and a single word void of pictorial support is capable of profound expression. Simple and straightforward typographic statements provide memorable images that awaken the mind and imagination of the reader. In a mere word, this *Time* cover effectively portrays the sinister presence of evil. Upon seeing the magazine on the newsstand, the word poses a penetrating question that for the potential reader must be answered.

Weekly news magazine

Typefaces possess visual characteristics that support, expand, and clarify the content of the words they represent. They have personalities and attitudes; they are capable of wide-ranging expression. On this *Time* cover, letters set in Times Roman form the word *EVIL*. The imposing size of the word and the sharp features of the pointed *v* and dracula-like serifs intensify the idea of evil. The indeterminate grey-on-black color evokes the question, "Does it exist—or do bad things just happen?" (left).

JUNE 10, 1991 $2.50

TIME

**Does it exist — or
do bad things just happen?**

0 724404

Color is a typographic element that deserves special consideration, for it is capable of contributing to the impact of a message. Observe how perceptions of the word *evil* change as different colors are applied to the word and its background (below).

Selecting typefaces for specific purposes is not an arbitrary task. Matching form and content requires an eye for detail and a talent for interpretation. Consider the typeface/word (form/content) marriages below.

Evil

Evil

Evil

Variex — **HappY**

Zapf Chancery — *depressed*

Industria — envious

Garamond 3 — intelligent

Snell Roundhand — *passionate*

Motion — jealous

Futura — neurotic

When the visual qualities of letters and words mimic verbal meaning, a verbal/visual equation is created. Often these equations are accomplished through simplified type manipulations, such as shifting letters, use of different type weights and italics, and altering sizes of letters. Verbal/visual equations can provide effective display settings such as titles, headlines, and other expressive applications.

exp a **n** d

singl e

sep **ar** ate

incomplet

a

m b

i

u

g

pr(e)gnant

u

s

o

W

O

r

g

run

jum p

**Designer:
Willi Kunz**

Abstract documents architecture projects by students from the School of Architecture, Planning, and Preservation at Columbia University. In keeping with the theme of the book, the pages appear "constructed" through the use of rectilinear divisions of space. The use of bold black and white shapes and typographic rules of varying weights establishes partitions for the information. Dynamic visual contrasts suggest three-dimensional space and the illusion of walking through an architectural setting. Remaining one of the most versatile typefaces since the 1950's, Univers provides the font variations and architectonic qualities necessary for this publication. An understanding and appreciation of Univers's geometric visual qualities will aid a designer in using the typeface effectively in any situation.

Abstract is published annually as a series, and for this reason the same design is used from year to year. The general design from issue to issue remains constant, but the flexibility of the system enables limitless visual possibilities. On the cover, for example, the title typography remains the same size, but its orientation to the page changes in response to featured architectural photographs (above, above right, and opposite page, top).

When designing a publication issued as a series, work out a design that is consistent from issue to issue, capable of change and visual diversity. Don't trap yourself into too rigid a system.

On the title of the cover, the letters of the word *ABSTRACT* touch, achieving the compact appearance of a logotype. Negative letter spacing is a device reserved for special display type situations such as this. Another device used on the cover superimposes an architectural drawing onto the title (above left). This technique is effectively used here, for it adds to the visual impact of the title. However, it is a technique to be used with prudence, as readability can be compromised and the visual integrity of the letterforms destroyed.

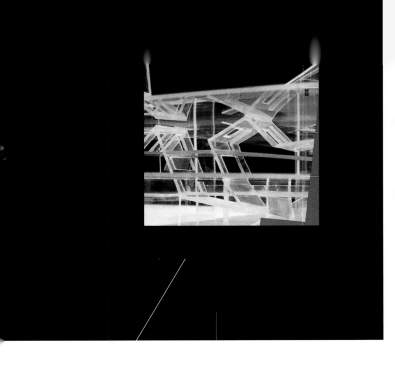

The symposium entitled "Critical Writings on Piranesi in America," was the textual installment of our exhibition on Piranesi as seen through the avant-garde "eye" of comtemporary theorists, architects, and historians. Participants included Diana Agrest, Stanley Allen, Jennifer Bloomer, the late Robin Evans, and Robin Middleton. The symposium "Modernism without Dogma: Architects of a Younger Generation in the Netherlands," showcased the works of Wiel Arets/Wim van den Bergh, Jan Benthem/Mels Crouwel, Mecanno, Ben van Berkel and others. The symposium's participants included Hans Ibelings curator of the exhibition, Francine Houben of Mecanno, Mels Crouwel, Ben van Berkel and Kenneth Frampton.

This detail of a text column reveals a high degree of craftsmanship and attention to detail. The column width, which corresponds to the grid, measures 12.5 picas. The type is set in 8/10 Univers 55. Two points of lead for a sans serif typeface such as Univers makes for comfortable reading and distinct, uncrowded lines of type. The rag of the column is near perfect with a feathery quality attained by balancing long and short lines. In order to control rags, it is necessary to judiciously hyphenate words, shift small words from one line to the next, or both. These are details that we as designers are now responsible for. In the age of desktop computers, designers also wear the hat of typesetter, a job once relinquished to a compositor in a type shop.

Each page is an intricate exploration of space. Often, as illustrated in the spread below, the space is divided into broad fields of black and white. The effect is a crisp and dramatic visual environment. The division of space is not unlike that of letterforms, where bold black and white shapes interact at their edges. The letter *A* to the right possesses the same magic and luminance as the spread below. On a practical note, letters clothed in black and white are easier to read than those appearing in other color combinations, for we are most accustomed to seeing them in this way.

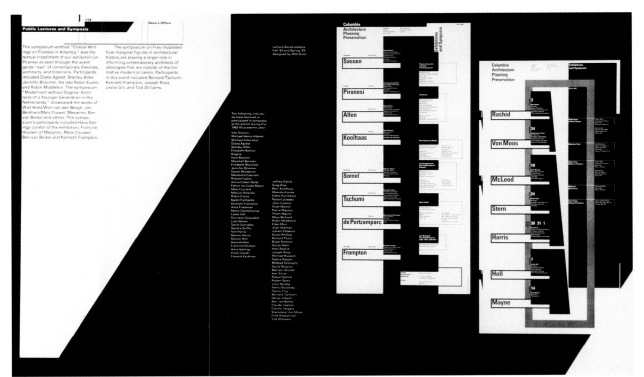

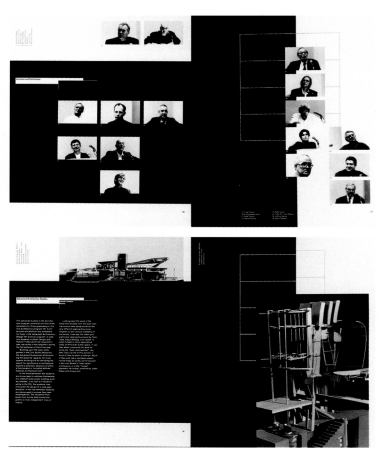

The pages of the book function as architectural metaphors. They simulate the qualities found in architectural spaces and define the structured environment for the organization of information. The typography is "built" by dividing the space into partitions containing various parts of information.

Typographic support elements, such as ruled lines and shapes, help organize the information into distinguishable units. Grids provide a general framework for the organization, but they are flexible grids that enable many variations.

The single most important principle in typography is contrast. Only when typographic elements oppose one another visually do they attain value. A bold letterform, for example, may stand for a headline while a light letterform stands for text. If contrast is sufficient, a reader clearly knows how to negotiate the information on the page. Contrasts are always a matter of

comparison: black/white, light/dark, thick/thin, serif/sans serif, large/small, round/square, etc. Compare the contrast between Univers 67 and 57, and Univers 57 and 57 Oblique (left). Compare the two sets of heads and subheads corresponding to these variants (right). The top right example, appearing in an issue of *Abstract*, clearly provides the most contrast.

a a

a *a*

The Shape of Two Cities:
New York-Paris Program

The Shape of Two Cities:
New York-Paris Program

Core Architecture Studios

23

Studio II

Spring '93

Lauretta Vinciarelli
Studio critic

The two projects are an introduction to the architecture of the city. They focus on two typical aspects of New York: the building as part of the fabric of the block, and the transit infrastructure as a punctuation in the movement of the city.

Ferry Terminal
Joe Crawford, M Arch, 3
Onyeije Nwokorie
M Arch, 2
Peter Rosenbaum
M Arch, 1

New York-Paris Program

Paris Studio	Spring '94	**Christian Biecher,** **Alain Salomon** **Studio critics**	*Library* Emmannelle Bourlier, 1 2	*Photography Center* Josh Birdsall, 3

Macro structures refer to the organization of the parts to the whole; micro structures refer to the organization of the parts. This series of books contain micro structures that organize detailed information

in much the same way that a well-organized drawer organizes utensils. These most often appear on the borders of the page and are composed of ruled lines and bars of varied weight that

enclose and separate parts of information. Two representative examples appear here. Notice how the microstructures form customized compartments for the typographic units.

The flexibility of this typographic system is quite evident in this spread, where text columns run both horizontally and vertically. Adding fuel to the visual dynamics of the page and the interplay of contrasts is text appearing as both white on a black background and black on a white background.

New York Paris Program
Paris Studio

Taking on the semester spent in New York, the Paris studio focused on the complementary notions of modern space and vernacular urban fabric of Paris. Divided in three different exercises, the course proposed a gradual exploration of those two themes. The first exercise was articulated around the Colin Rowe essay,

"Transparency: Literal and Phenomenal." The students were asked to design the model of a space derived from their personal reading of the text. This new experience was then transformed into a more traditional architecture problem, that was to be the design of a photography center, located in a very artistic neighborhood of the Paris rive gauche, where

all the experiments on transparency had to make sense within a program articulated around…dark rooms. This second exercise made the students sensitive to the simple fabric of a homogeneous area. As students became more aware of the Parisian fabric, especially through classes such as History of Paris, the third

exercise put them into the difficult situation of having to design a neighborhood library on a difficult triangular site located on the Hauss-mannian rue Lafayette. Referring to both the vivid French contemporary architecture and the Parisian urban fabric, the studio course was inviting to a complete design experience.

The Shape of Two Cities:
New York Paris Program

Beatriz Seidler, Meredith Sykes
Directors

The Shape of Two Cities Program is designed to develop a student's critical appreciation of urban form, its genesis, and the role of architecture, preservation, and planning in the creation of the contemporary urban environment. The program provides a year-long introduction to the disciplines of architecture, urbanism, planning and preservation for highly motivated undergraduates who have completed at least two years of study at their home institutions. Previous study in these disciplines is not a requirement of admission to the program. The program's curriculum is designed to provide students with a better understanding of the design disciplines as they are practiced in both New York and Paris. New York and Paris are highly unique cities, each representative of its individual cultures. For students these cities offer an ideal opportunity to explore the historical, social and political development of urban form, and to clarify the roles of architects, planners and preservationists upon it. The program offers thirty-two course credits which are applicable towards Bachelor of Arts degrees granted by participating institutions. Further, the program provides an excellent preparation for graduate and professional study.

During the first semester the students are enrolled at the Graduate School of Architecture, Planning and Preservation and enjoy the resources of the School and Columbia University. In the following semester students are based at the School's academic and classroom facility, in Paris' historic Marais district, under the tutelage of the program's co-director, Meredith Sykes. The program is divided into two divisions, Architecture and Planning/Preservation, with a core curriculum which supports both divisions. The core curriculum provides a critical analytic model with which to interpret the development of urban form, consists of lecture courses and seminars, helping ground design research projects in the physical, intellectual, historical and cultural contexts of both New York and Paris. Course work is supplemented by visiting lecturers and critics representing both the professional and academic communities in each city. Students who elect the Architecture Option will pursue a series of increasingly complex studio projects which focus on the analysis, creation and representation of urban architecture. For Planning/Preservation students seminar papers in the first semester are assigned in preparation for an extensive research project in Paris, developed under the guidance of the faculty.

The Shape of Two Cities draws students from over thirty-six colleges and universities across the nation, with many schools electing to participate each year. Enrollment is limited to 35 students. Upon graduating from their respective institutions, many students are admitted to graduate programs in architecture, urban planning, and historic preservation at universities including Columbia, Harvard, M.I.T., Pennsylvania, and Yale.

Amherst College
Bates College
Brown University
Colby College
Creighton University
Dillard University
Duke University
Emory University
Fordham University
Franklin and Marshall College
Goucher College
Harvard University
Hobart College
Johns Hopkins University
Lehigh University
McGill University

Middlebury College
Oberlin College
Sarah Lawrence College
Skidmore College
Smith College
Stanford University
Trinity College
Tufts University
University of Michigan
University of Pennsylvania
University of Virginia
Vanderbilt University
Vassar College
Washington University
Wesleyan University
Williams College
Williams Smith College
Yale University

Christian Biecher
Alain Salomon
Studio critics

Library
Emmanuelle Bourlier, 1/2
Paris Student 3

Designers:
**Craig Minor
Cheryl Brzezinski-
Beckett**

The designers of *Cite,* the architecture and design review of Houston, were faced with a very common design problem concerning how to fit an overabundance of text into the publication without making it look too busy, clumsy, and crowded. To solve this problem, they chose Sabon as the primary text type because of its narrow set width and light visual appearance. Several other typefaces join Sabon to visually support the publication's theme which focuses on Texas-Tamaulipas border culture and architecture. These include Journal, Orator, Template Gothic, and Ribbon 131. These vernacular typefaces express the enigmatic qualities associated with life "on the border."

The magazine cover is divided into halves. The top half contains a photograph of downtown Laredo, Texas; the bottom half houses typography announcing feature stories. Note the careful placement of the title *Cite* set in robust Times Roman letters. The horizontal stroke of the lower-case *e* precisely matches the edge of the photograph. When you are making detailed adjustments such as this, magnify the type to at least 400%. Working at a lesser percentage will not ensure accuracy in the final output.

The textural typography located at the bottom of the cover possesses qualities not unlike the hand-painted letters on the building in the photograph. Each possesses a rather haphazard, informal quality and a distinct verticality due to the use of condensed letterforms. To achieve this effect, the designers set the lines of type in Univers Ultra Light Condensed. The lines were then selected, letter spaced, and positioned individually for an effective, asymmetrical arrangement. Notice also that the words *ON THE BORDER* literally appear on the "border" of the magazine's cover. This technique provides an excellent example of how a publication's content affects the choice of typeface and its spatial arrangement.

When setting display type, the computer does not automatically space letters as you might desire. The top example displays the title *Cite* set with normal letter spacing. The designers of the magazine, however, desiring a bolder and more consolidated word unit, reduced the letter spacing by tracking the word to achieve the desired effect (middle). Spacing in the bottom example is pushed beyond the acceptable limit. Notice the ugly shapes and the awkward crowded letters. Unless you are creating a special visual effect with touching or overlapping letters, it is best to provide enough space between them so that they can breathe. Without adequate letter spacing, readability is greatly reduced.

The designers of *Cite* chose Univers Ultra Condensed, all capitals for the contents page because of its distinct, vertical posture and bold weight (top). Compare the weight of this face with the weights of two other Univers Condensed faces, light and thin. Each weight possesses a different stroke-to-height ratio, a proportional characteristic that affects the width of the letters. While the letters shown here are all the same height, they appear progressively condensed due to lighter stroke weights.

HOUSTON MEETS BERLIN
HOUSTON MEETS BERLIN
HOUSTON MEETS BERLIN

t o

n

On the magazine's contents page, the cover title is repeated at the same size but changed to a light shade of gray. Screening type is an effective way to create variety, emphasis, and the illusion of three dimensions. The lighter the value, the more a form appears to recede in space and vice versa. Four shades of gray are shown here at 90%, 60%, 20%, and 5% (from top to bottom).

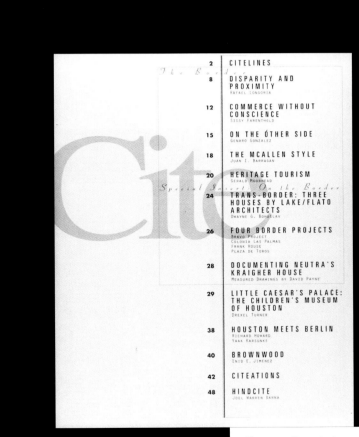

2 | CITELINES

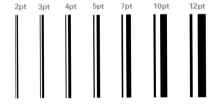

2pt 3pt 4pt 5pt 7pt 10pt 12pt

Separating article titles and authors on the contents page is a 4-point combination rule joined to a thin horizontal rule at right angles (see detail above). This provides emphasis to the titles and separates them from the adjacent page numbers. Notice that the size of this combination rule was chosen because its heavier line matches the width of the letter strokes. This is a subtle yet important distinction. The computer enables you to assign any weight to rules, but visual sensitivity should guide your decisions.

The type on the contents page repeats the theme of the cover. Because the article titles are set in letter spaced Univers Ultra Condensed in all capitals, a memorable texture is created, but readability is sacrificed to a degree. This is probably appropriate since there is only a small amount of copy and the letters appear as display type.

THE TEXA

LITTLE CAE

BERLIN MEETS

PULL-OUT

Learning the specific characteristics of typefaces and possessing the ability to distinguish one from the next is a challenge for anyone working with type. Having this ability provides the designer with the knowledge to select just the right fonts for any application. Sometimes the differences in fonts are very subtle, as in the examples to the right. At first glance you may find the fonts to appear the same, but upon closer inspection you will see many differences between them. For example, look at the lower-case *e* and *g* and the uppercase *W* in each font. What similarities and differences do you find in these fonts? Sabon (top), Caslon 540 (middle), and Times New Roman (bottom).

Some political change came about with the November 1992 elections. President Clinton in his State of the Union address spoke again in favor of additional legislation that would protect the environment and workers and protect against the "import surge" that could result from the

Some political change came about with the November 1992 elections. President Clinton in his State of the Union address spoke again in favor of additional legislation that would protect the environment and workers and protect against the "import surge" that could result from the

Some political change came about with the November 1992 elections. President Clinton in his State of the Union address spoke again in favor of additional legislation that would protect the environment and workers and protect against the "import surge" that could result from the

The display typeface Template Gothic abounds with odd proportions, peculiar shapes, and eccentricities. There exists something unresolved and askew about the face – qualities befitting the subject matter of the Mexican-American border culture.

Notable traits of Template Gothic include rounded stroke terminals that also come to a point in letters such as *T* and *R*, a truncated stroke in the letter *e*, and a substantially heavier stroke on the right side of the letter *O* than on the left (see spread opposite page).

The stretch of the Río Bravo–Rio Grande and its environs that encompasses the area from Laredo–Nuevo Laredo to Brownsville-Matamoros is only a brief span of the 2,000-mile border between Mexico and the United States. But this region is more

The stretch of the Río Bravo–Rio Grande and its environs that encompasses the area from Laredo–Nuevo Laredo to Brownsville-Matamoros is only a brief span of the 2,000-mile border between Mexico and the United States. But this region is more

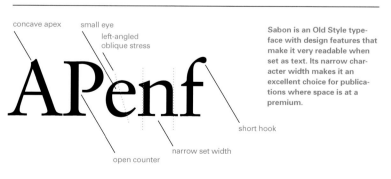

concave apex

small eye

left-angled oblique stress

short hook

narrow set width

open counter

Sabon is an Old Style typeface with design features that make it very readable when set as text. Its narrow character width makes it an excellent choice for publications where space is at a premium.

The traditional use of drop caps to mark article openings contrasts well with non-traditional typographic treatments. This 5-line drop cap was generated by simply inputting the desired paragraph specifications. The computer automatically aligns the drop cap to the adjacent lines of text. Sizing

adjustments should be made to ensure correct optical adjustment. The drop cap in the top example appears visually higher than the text. The bottom example reflects a slight reduction in the size of the drop cap (97%) for a more sensitive optical alignment.

On the Other Side

The magazine contains thin rules at the head and foot of each page. These enclose the type and images and provide a system for designing running heads. Since these rules appear on every page, they are placed on a document master page along with the folios and other recurring items. The pages capture attention with dynamic scale contrasts in the photographs and display type. The use of several different display typefaces throughout the magazine creates stunning visual variety.

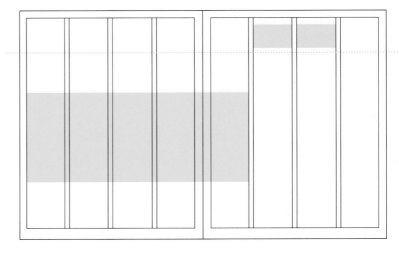

Commerce Without Conscience

SISSY FARENTHOLD

The display type for article openings changes from article to article. Here, a rough-hewn, typewriter-like font called Journal was carefully chosen to relate visually to the slums pictured in the photograph. The computer becomes an extremely powerful tool for selecting and arranging display type, for on the monitor you can try different fonts, visually assess their effectiveness and adjust their size and spacing.

The tabloid-size magazine is organized on the basis of a standard four-column grid to which the text type strictly adheres. The grid features 13.5 pica columns separated by intervals of 1.25 picas. This provides a measure to accommodate approximately 40 characters of 9-point Sabon text type per line for optimum readability. Lines are separated with 3 points of lead. All page composition software enables you to make grids for your designs. This provides a framework or skeleton for the organization of the type and images. Compare the actual page (above) to its grid (bottom). The yellow rectangles represent the placements of the photographs; the blue dotted line is a flow line, which is a guide line indicating where the text begins on each page.

Designer:
Aleš Najbrt

Raut, a word meaning a "soiree with the best and brightest," transcends the limitations of the typical magazine format. The reproductions of the magazine's covers and spreads pictured here do not adequately represent the impact of its size and the fragrance of its contents. Measuring 18.75" x 26.75", the magazine is more akin to a series of bound posters. *Raut* presents through intoxicating, larger-than-life photography and probing typography, the lives and works of creative individuals. The magazine should be visited and absorbed as if a gallery space. Readers are guests, invited not as casual observers, but as active participants in creative discourse.

The grandiose photographs dominating the covers of *Raut* reveal a monumentality rarely observed in contemporary magazine design. The animated letters forming the masthead are a fascinating blend of curvilinear and rectilinear strokes, a combination which establishes a unified and distinctively playful title. These letters suggest human stick figures with flat serifs resembling hands and feet.

Raut's editor-in-chief and designer, Aleš Najbrt, is also a designer of typefaces, many of which appear in the publication. The font shown here, Prague Five Bold, is vivid, angular, and wonderfully eccentric – qualities that also render the magazine so engaging. This typeface may be seen in the two covers above for the contents of the magazine.

The cover on the opposite page achieves impact through a dynamic combination of type and image. A photograph of a woman with a piercing glance, cropped, sized, angled, and bled off the edges of the cover, slightly overlaps the masthead. The magazine contents, set in letter spaced Prague Five Bold, opposite the woman's right eye is a delicate counterpoint to the bold and vibrant image. Separation of type and image permits each to function without interference from the other. When they touch or overlap in unexpected and effective ways, communicative power can be strengthened.

RAUT

ČERVENEC 96 JULY

73 – 96

SPOLEČENSKÝ VEČER VYBRANÉ S
SOIREE WITH THE BEST AND

NAČEVA

VLÁČIL

AUTOPSIA

ŠIK

BURBON

REKLAMY

TESAŘOVÁ

HAMPL

SESTRY VÁLOVY

RYČL

BOUDNÍK

NĚMEC

FOTO TONO STANO

TERESA A SPIRITU SANCTO

Gently curved lines of type hover over a portrait of a nun to suggest a halo (above). Similar expressive type treatments are found throughout issues of *Raut,* the example on the opposite page providing a good example. A text block with a distinctive, computer-generated shape is read and viewed in concert with type displaying other daring effects.

The pages of *Raut* follow no prescribed design formula or grid; design is driven entirely by content. Within a single issue, type is set in a myriad of ways, from flush left, ragged right to centered, justified, and irregularly-shaped text blocks. To explore the spirit of *Raut,* rules of legibility are often stretched to their outermost limits: text may extend across an entire page, or be set very small and dense and reversed out of a black background. Always, photography adds impact (see examples above and right).

Scotland Yard na stopě !

Scotland Yard on the trail !

A)DE SE NA RAUT!
LET'S GO TO RAUT!

Type can appear as a slight ripple on a pond or as a pounding ocean wave. With the aid of a computer and most available drawing programs, any number of circling, arcing, curving, and bending effects can be achieved. These effects are most successful when the designer's eye is attuned to readability, a quality largely determined by the tightness of a curve in relationship to the size of the type and the typeface used. Type improperly scaled on a tightly curved baseline causes characters to abruptly bump into each other (top). Smaller type on a similar curve flows smoothly and effortlessly (bottom). Type set on curved baselines reveals an infinite number of expressive possibilities (far right).

The hypothesis that there is an ideally correct form for each letter of the alphabet is just as erroneous as Geofroy Tory's

hypothesis

The hypothesis that there is an ideally correct

The hypothesis that there is an ideally

The hypothesis that there is an ideally correct form for each letter of the alphabet is just as erroneous as Geofroy Tory

Designer:
Amy Puglisi

The focus of this lifestyle magazine is healthful eating, drinking, cooking, socializing, and other domestic activities such as gardening. Built around the theme of a piazza, which is a public square in an Italian town, the magazine design draws on the cultural attributes associated with these public gathering places. The square is the central motif of the magazine, where it influences the magazine's structure and typographic treatments. Two primary type families are used throughout the publication: Modula for heads, call-outs, and captions; Garamond for text. These two families offer excellent contrast and provide the magazine with a fresh, upbeat, and elegant quality.

The structure of the magazine is based on the idea of a piazza or square. The magazine's cover, consisting of three panels and two folds, is die-cut with a large square. This wraps around the interior pages of the magazine, and when looking at the folded cover the reader sees but half of the square, positioned at the left edge. The title, *piazza*, printed on the first interior page, is revealed through the die-cut.

front cover (folded)

inside front cover, inside back cover, and third fold-in panel, also die-cut (unfolded)

The pattern gracing the magazine's cover was computer generated by repeating the letters z and a, screening the letters for a light tone, and superimposing a grid pattern of white squares over the letters to fracture and fragment them. The resulting effect resembles the cobblestones or bricks in a piazza. The black letters below represent their appearance before manipulation. The grey squares indicate the superimposed grid.

Most words possess some attribute that can be emphasized to achieve a meaningful and memorable visual effect and to suggest a particular sound quality. Within the word *piazza,* the proximity of two z characters produces a vibrating, diagonal pattern. These letters have been exaggerated with color, which places the stress on the two letters when the word is spoken. Look for such unusual characteristics in words to produce unusual visual and auditory effects.

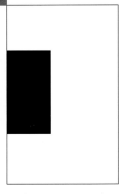

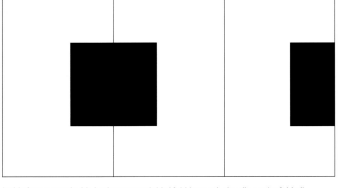

Details can make all the difference in how a typographic message is read and perceived. To stress the idea of *Life* in the word *Lifestyle,* a bolder version of Garamond is used.

Lifestyle Quarterly

When selecting a specific typeface for a publication, be aware that although fonts may have the same name and may be derived from the same original source, they more than likely have subtle (or not-so-subtle) differences in design. Compare Adobe Garamond, Garamond 3, and Stempel Garamond, all in 24 point (from top to bottom). Adobe Garamond is the type family used in this magazine.

garamond
garamond
garamond

Lifestyle Quarterly
piazza
Spring 1995

The cover of piazza effectively combines solid color, pattern, and minimal typography for a polished and cultivated appearance.

Contributing to the visual opulence of the magazine, large, ghosted photographs serving as backgrounds for type and other images, extend beyond page boundaries. These photographs must appear light enough to secure the readability of text type.

Coffee beans do not grow underground, but begin as flowers on trees. Each flower has two seeds, one of which is the coffee bean. The beans turn **bright red** when they are ripe. After they are picked and dried, they are ready for roasting and brewing.

A sidebar about how coffee is grown overlaps an image of coffee beans. At the point of overlap, the photograph is lightened (indicated in the diagram to the left as a lighter grey) to preserve the readability of the type. The words *bright red* are enlarged and printed in red to demonstrate their meaning. The lines of type in the bold sidebar align with those in the adjacent text block, giving the page visual cohesiveness.

A headline announcing a recipe sends a double message. Enlarging the letters *eat* in the word *feature* creates two words from one. Typographic riddles such as this are entertaining as well as informative.

fEATure FOOD
biscotti

The running text in the publication is set justified to preserve the squarish shape of the piazza theme. Ragged text does not possess the rectilinear character of justified text. Set in 9/26 Garamond, the plentiful line spacing is at the same time posh and readable.

Many people see large glass jars of these elongated toast-like delicacies in the corner coffee shop, but don't know what they are or more importantly—what to do with them. A singular one is called biscotto, two or more are called biscotti. They are crisp Italian cookies flavored with anise and often contain almonds or filberts.

As a central design motif, the square is reintroduced in different ways throughout the magazine. This can be seen in text type, color, and photographs that mimic the size and position of the square on the cover; letters cropped within square shapes (see spreads below); and in details such as the table of contents where page numbers are "squared-off" by cropping them at the bottom (below).

If for a special effect you wish to crop letters as in the spread below, remember that the recognizability of the letter is dependent upon the manner by which it is cropped. If you wish for the letter to be identified by the reader, reveal those parts of its anatomy that distinguish it from all other letters. Below, the letter *e* is shown with various croppings. some more readable than others.

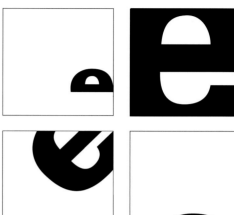

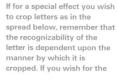

your most direct interaction with the earth

Designers:
Katie Salen
Barbara Foley
Sonya Mead
Karen White

Zed is an interdisciplinary journal bridging the gap between designer, student, and educator. It is a vehicle for the cross-fertilization of ideas and divergent view-points, and its design resounds with a similar attitude and commitment. The word *Zed* is English in origin, meaning the letter z, and it is the expression of the commitment the journal has to alternative ideas. There resides in the journal's name the implication of addressing a full range of information, from a through z. The shape of the letter *z* with its diagonal stroke linking opposite horizontal strokes suggests bridging ideological gaps. While expressive and experimental in form and content, the journal nonetheless retains a normative edge, responding to those principles that make type readable.

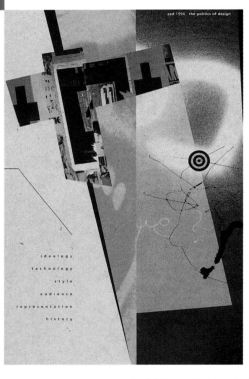

In the page presented below, translucent pages are printed on both sides, folded in half, and bound into the journal. Upon turning the pages, the reader is able to see only a faint shadow of the elements printed on the inside of the sheet. But these ghostlike types and images complement the more visually distinct typographic elements on the outside of the sheet. Shown below is an introduction page.

The two primary typefaces used for *Zed* are Interstate and Frutiger, both sans serif. A casual glance at the two faces may reveal little difference between them; however, closer examination discloses subtle variance in form. It is usually best to select typefaces that contrast greatly from one another so as to easily distinguish them and their assigned function on the page. Perhaps the choice of these two typefaces supports the underlying premise of Zed – an open consideration of alternative design methods and means. Compare representative letters from Interstate (top) and Frutiger (bottom) fonts.

aegw
aegw

Unlike the average scholarly journal, *Zed* articulates its content through a design that is richly varied in structure, rhythm, and texture. Typography teams with photographic images and montages to deliver the content in a visually seductive, poetic manner. These characteristics are readily observed on the cover (above). Note the modest and understated typography used for the title and content listings. These elements blend with the imagery rather than boastfully commanding authority over it.

A list of design themes covered in the journal appear as subtitles on the cover. The importance of these themes is established in the dramatic letter spacing, which provides a distinctive texture and emphasis. The interval of space between the letters sends a message to the reader that the words should be enunciated, read slowly, and pondered. Added space between letters within words slows the eye, and therefore the reading process. Compare the letter spaced words as they appear on the cover (far left) with those set normally (left).

i d e o l o g y

t e c h n o l o g y

s t y l e

a u d i e n c e   ideology

r e p r e s e n t a t i o n   technology

h i s t o r y   style

audience

representation

history

The Popularity of Social Issues in Design: Learning from Emerging Patterns

Matthew Monk

Political, social, and environmental issues surround our society. Working in a climate saturated by such concerns, the graphic designer faces an escalating challenge to deal with such issues productively.

This climate of social awareness coincides with an important stage in the development of the graphic design profession. As designers struggle to define and better articulate the profession, and as we continue to gain the power to influence content in design, social and political issues become an increasingly important factor.

But use of these topics has reached an extremely fashionable level that places them in jeopardy; without careful and responsible attention from designers, audiences will grow weary of these important issues. The question then becomes: How can designers responsibly incorporate social, political, and environmental concerns into their work?

This article critiques some emerging patterns in the way designers address important social issues with an emphasis on discussing and analyzing some common destructive design practices. In analyzing these patterns, the article draws conclusions for helping the design community embrace these issues and address them responsibly and productively.

In reading and viewing *Zed,* one is confronted continually with visual anomalies that call into question established typographic practice. Trapezoidal text blocks constructed of divergent angles, for example, suggest new directions, new typographic alternatives. What makes the text in *Zed* so unusual is the fact that we are accustomed to seeing text as rectangular shapes, and departures from this convention strike us as being somewhat peculiar. Despite this departure, *Zed's* text is highly readable. It is crafted in 7.2/12 Interstate, a legible sans serif face with a narrow set width. Even though the text block is justified in alignment, it appears consistent in color, and the generous line spacing contributes to its readability. Within the text, selected elements are set in Interstate Bold for emphasis.

Political, social, and environmental issues surround our society. Working in a climate saturated by such concerns, the graphic designer faces an escalating challenge to deal with such issues productively.

This climate of social awareness coincides with an important stage in the development of the graphic design profession. As designers struggle to define and better articulate the profession, and as we continue to gain the power to influence content in design, social and political issues become an increasingly important factor.

But use of these topics has reached an extremely fashionable level that places them in jeopardy; **without careful and responsible attention from designers,** audiences will grow weary of these important issues. The question then becomes: **How can designers responsibly incorporate social, political, and environmental concerns into their work?**

This article critiques some emerging patterns in the way designers address important social issues with an emphasis on discussing and analyzing some common destructive design practices. In analyzing these patterns, the article draws conclusions for helping the design community embrace these issues and address them responsibly and productively.

Related to the general theme, "the politics of design," typography is integrated with evocative montages of photographs featuring grafitti and other public messages. The imagery and typography correspond in their angular, wedge-like shapes, a marriage that visually unifies the active page.

17

A central design motif recurring throughout the publication is a graphic target, representing the focused pursuit of ideas. It is used in conjunction with the page numbers as an indexing icon. As the reader progresses from section to section through the journal, the white arrow piercing the target rotates in a clockwise direction. This flip-book device signifies time-based media.

The angled text blocks are created by running a normal text block around a wedge shape such as the one shown to the upper right in grey. The angle of the wedge determines the angled edge of the text block.

Zed pages frequently consist of several irregularly shaped text blocks and other angled type elements that give the reader an unsettled feeling. Yet all of the elements on the page are arranged with sensitivity to asymmetrical composition.

[**politics of ideology**]

A photograph and black bar combine with typography to create an effective headline configuration. On a practical note, when reversing type from a photograph, be sure there is enough contrast between the type and the photo to preserve readability.

Designer:
Banu Berker

This design of *Artsword,* the Penn State School of Visual Arts newsletter, offers an Alice-in-Wonderland adventure into the world of typographic form. The visual energy radiating from the pages is a direct result of using the computer as a design tool (not just a production tool) to explore typographic possibilities. For example, headlines appear as mini-constructivist paintings, and odd but surprising words are created by combining different typefaces for emphasis. Although typographic conventions are stretched to the limit, the newsletter remains readable for an audience of artists and designers accustomed to alternative ideas and images. Bending rules is appropriate when the designer keeps in sight the aims of the project and the needs and nature of the audience.

ARtsword

A rather cacophonic assemblage of typographic forms and images dazzles the cover. Photographs mingle with heavy black rectilinear shapes, framing a space for a letter from the director of the school. The letter's typography consists of single, very long, well-spaced lines of type. Though the length of the lines exceeds the character count recommended for optimum readability, the brevity of the letter makes reading tolerable. Also, the device of emphasizing specific terms by means of different typefaces, weights, and sizes helps to capture the attention of readers (right).

The newsletter title, which forms the masthead, is a constructed motif composed of Garamond and Univers letters in a balanced field of black and white rectilinear shapes. The visual oddities of the title provide a complex but intriguing word picture. *Arts* is composed of Garamond capitals with only the *t* appearing in lower-case; *word* is composed entirely of lower-case letters the same height as the capitals. This, along with the green letter *w* establishing the visual center of the title, provides compositional unity (above).

Key words from the director's letter featured on the cover combine Futura Bold lower-case letters and Futura Bold Small Capitals. This two-part division provides the reader with the essential meaning of the words and activates them on the page. For example, installation reads (install)a-tion, and reunion reads re(union). Be aware that some typefaces such as Futura do not include small caps in their families. Creating Futura small capitals is accomplished with a computer command that renders lower-case letters as small capitals. Whenever possible, use small capitals specifically designed for type families (below).

INSTALLation

DESIGN

EDUCATIONal

reUNION

These two pages display the extraordinary typographical variety achieved in the newsletter. Within a loosely structured two-column grid, it appears as if the type is painted onto the pages. This is particularly true of the red page, which is an expressive interpretation of a provocative anonymous letter left on the desk of a faculty member. Different fonts, type sizes, shapes, ruled lines, and spacings are freely explored with the computer. Words contained within the letter visually reveal the passion of the author (left).

Numerals and letters of different sizes are reversed from a square and dynamically arranged to create a sign representing various decades (left).

The spirit of artistic play is apparent in article headlines. In this example, the words composing the headline are positioned into an animated display that transforms them into a picture (below).

The newsletter utilizes various ways of emphasizing words or phrases within text. One method is shown in the top example. Other variations on this theme explore different uses of the ruled lines, color, and backgrounds (below).

Prints by Fayette campus' **David DiPietro** were selected for the 1993

Prints by Fayette campus' **David DiPietro** were selected for the 1993

Prints by Fayette campus' **David DiPietro** were selected for the 1993

Prints by Fayette campus' **David DiPietro** were selected for the 1993

Prints by Fayette campus' **David DiPietro** were selected for the 1993

Prints by Fayette campus' **David DiPietro** were selected for the 1993

Art Educator Finds Cultural Colonialism in West Virginia

by R. Stephen Carpenter

Designer:
Harold Burch

Corporate newsletter

The cover of this issue of *Currents,* the internal newsletter for Warner Communications Inc., replicates El Lissitzky's famous poster "Beat the Whites with the Red Wedge." (Small type at the bottom of the cover offers apologies to El Lissitzky and assurance to the reader that the visual mimicry is purely metaphorical.) Whereas in the original poster the red wedge (Bolshevik Army) slashes through the white circle (Kerenski's forces) for a graphic statement about the 1917 October Revolution, on the cover the red wedge points to the image of a record, thus introducing the feature article about Elektra Records. Inside the newsletter, bold typographic rules further suggest El Lissitzky's constructions. Futura, the sans serif typeface designed by Paul Renner in 1927, functions as the text type and complements the geometric shapes composing the cover.

The original poster, *Beat the Whites with the Red Wedge,* 1919, by El Lissitzky.

The legibility of typefaces is not based upon standardized criterion. Some designers still follow conventional wisdom in believing that serif typefaces are more legible. However, legibility boils down to what readers have become accustomed to over time, and with an increase over the decades in the design and use of sans serif designs, there is no distinguishable difference in the legibility of these two type classifications. Sans-serif typefaces can be extremely legible (some more than others). Compare two classics: Futura, the typeface used in this publication, and Times. Which is more legible?

Futura
Times

The only consistent thing about this newsletter is the fact that nothing is consistent. Every cover and every interior possesses a unique design, and as a result the newsletter is highly experimental in nature. The typography and design vary enormously from issue to issue, a freedom in approach that certainly inspired the El Lissitzky theme characterizing the cover (above).

These four rectangles mimic similar forms found on the El Lissitzky poster and serve as a large initial *E* that introduces the feature story (see spread below). When

used appropriately, custom designed letterforms can be highly effective on the page.

We're not interested in setting trends, starting trends, or following trends. We're interested in being the best. Choosing the best talent. That's the only trend we're involved in.

Heavy, 5-point rule lines separate lines of text from the rest of the article, a method for creating sidebars that is reminiscent of Russian Constructivist typography from the early part of the twentieth century, and especially the pages in *The Isms of Art,* designed by El Lissitzky in 1924. You can bring life to the text of your publications by creating sidebars such as this.

The hypothesis that there is an ideally correct form for each letter of the alphabet is just as erroneous as Geofroy Tory's

The hypothesis that there is an ideally correct form for each letter of the alphabet is just as erroneous as Geofroy

The newsletter text, set justified in 10/14 Futura on a 10-pica measure, appears quite easy to read. Adding a few more characters per line would make it even better. The readability of the text is improved because words are hyphenated to reduce the number of awkward gaps between characters and words. Compare the improved spacing of the justified text column set with hyphenation (far left) with the spacing of the column set without hyphenation (left).

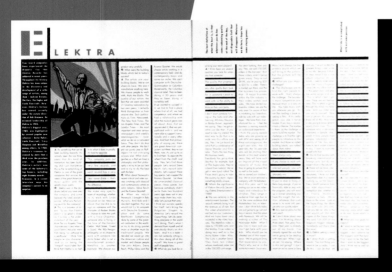

An interior spread of the newsletter consists of a 5-column grid. Each column is separated and framed by prominent black rule lines. The text settings fall below a flowline marked by a thick bar rule. The white space above the flowline lightens an otherwise very full page, and provides a division of space that creates pleasing spatial proportions.

The article featured in the spread above consists of a question and answer interview. Special dingbats were created to identify the "questions" and "answers." Not only do these icons make it easy for the reader to follow the interview, they expand the metaphorical theme of the newsletter and surprise the text with welcome company.

Designers:
Anne Bush
Karen White

A cross between a poster and a newsletter, this publication provides information about the Department of Art at the University of Hawaii at Manoa, and announces a series of visual arts lectures for the public. Vivid, silhouetted palm trees, mysterious photographic images, and expressive typography commingle to reinforce the theme of the lecture series, *intersections*. This theme, which suggests Hawaii's diverse society and culture and the meeting of minds from various parts of the world, is represented by a number of typographic devices. Grid lines, for example, suggest Hawaii's location in a map of converging latitude and longitude lines ("somewhere between the tropic of cancer and the tropic of capricorn"), and lines of type converge, overlap, flip-flop, and intersect.

94–95

intersections

...where between the tropic of cancer and the tropic of capricorn

In a painterly manner, the computer is used to create and juxtapose positive, negative, and colored type elements.

This newsletter/poster is printed on two sides of a single sheet of paper, and folded in half twice. Some of the elements, including the expansive photomontage and the display typography, are repeated on both sides of the sheet. On one side, however, these components are flip-flopped, appearing upside-down and backwards. The inverted display type can be read, but functions more as image than word. The text type on this page is also inverted, having been set flush right, ragged left as opposed to its alignment on the opposite side, which is flush left, ragged right. The effect of these visual maneuvers is the illusion that the paper is transparent, enabling the reader to see through to the opposite side. This front/back interaction further stresses the "intersection" theme. Compare the two sides of the publication shown on this spread.

Continually trying to find new ways of configuring typography to make it both more visual and more readable is a worthy goal of anyone working with type. Here, by lowering the yellow dates set flush-right in relation to the names set flush-left, rather than aligning them on the same baseline, a syncopated rhythm emerges. Also, setting this text type on a black background provides a glowing brilliance.

11.17.94 **lucy lippard**

1.24.95 **elizabeth diller**

3.15.95 **edgar heap of birds**

4.5.95 **holly block**

* 5.95 **vaughn oliver**

Within this charged visual field, text type that must be easily read is for the most part treated with normative clarity. But in the spirit of experimentation, liberties are taken with color. In one instance, small text type is printed in yellow ink on a white background. The inability of the reader to distinguish the letters from the background inhibits readability. If you wish to assign a hue to text type, keep in mind that contrast between the type and its background is essential for optimum readability. The examples to the right offer varying degrees of readability, with the black text being the most readable.

The hypothesis that there is an ideally correct form for each letter of the alphabet is just as

The hypothesis that there is an ideally correct form for each letter of the alphabet is just as

The hypothesis that there is an ideally correct form for each letter of the alphabet is just as

The hypothesis that there is an ideally correct form for each letter of the alphabet is just as

The hypothesis that there is an ideally correct form for each letter of the alphabet is just as

The hypothesis that there is an ideally correct form for each letter of the alphabet is just as

university of hawai'i at manoa department of art

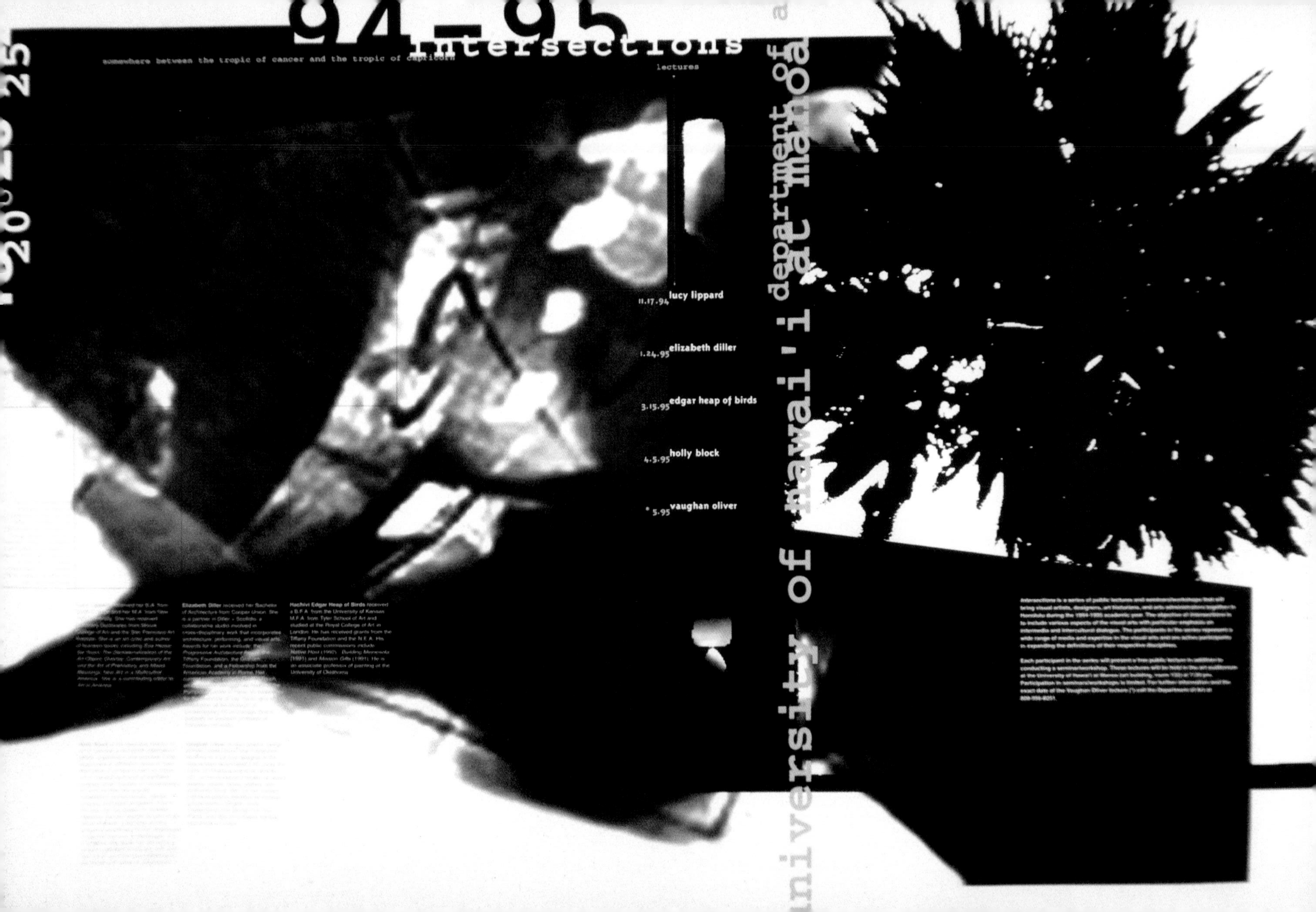

94-95 intersections

lectures

11.17.94 lucy lippard

1.24.95 elizabeth diller

3.15.95 edgar heap of birds

4.5.95 holly block

5.95 vaughan oliver

somewhere between the tropic of cancer and the tropic of capricorn

Designer:
Kristin Breslin Sommese

Assistant designer:
Jim Lilly

Many newsletters lull their readers to sleep. But when typographic designers intelligently select typefaces, understand their visual characteristics, and effectively manipulate them on the page, readers remain alert and read even the dullest information. This design of *Artsword* takes full advantage of the classical typeface Bodoni, utilizing varying sizes and weights to draw the reader into its pages. When set into text, Bodoni's crisp texture resonates, a by-product of the extreme contrast between the thick and thin strokes of the letters. This design, teetering on the edge of order and chaos, heightens reader interest and engages the intellect in a search for the underlying order.

B

Bodoni, the typeface used throughout the newsletter, is characterized by an extreme contrast between the thin and thick strokes of letters. Observe the delicate transitions from the thin to the thick strokes of the letter *B*. This provides a jewel-like, sparkling quality, and a distinct presence on the page when set into text. This version, produced by Bauer, is perhaps the closest in design to the original fonts designed by Giambattista Bodoni around 1790.

Non-Profit Organization

U.S. Postage

...paid

University Park, PA

permit **no. 1**

Taking full advantage of the visual qualities of Bodoni, the computer was used to manipulate letters into several engaging typographic configurations. Artfully scaling, grouping, and positioning letters lead to dynamic and varied type formations.

f c u l   N e W
A   ty   s

volume**1**, Number**1**, Fall 1993

Page 1 opens the newsletter with a letter set in a single, wide, generously-leaded column. Selected words and phrases are emphasized by changing the size of the type. This creates a lively visual pattern and an animated statement from the director of the school.

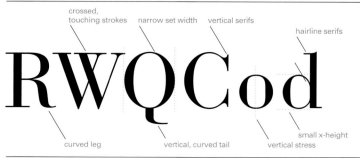

crossed, touching strokes
narrow set width
vertical serifs
hairline serifs

RWQCod

curved leg
vertical, curved tail
vertical stress
small x-height

Bodoni has been assigned the historical classification of a "modern" type family. The earmarks presented here are common among typefaces bearing this classification. These characteristics set Bodoni apart as one of the most beautiful and functional typefaces. You will find it an appropriate typeface choice for any number of purposes.

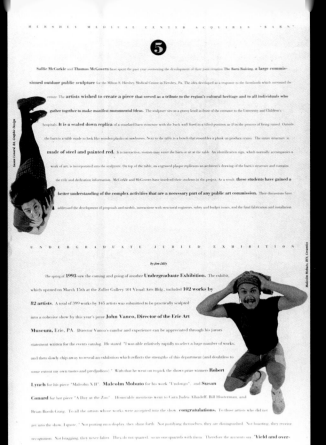

5

Sallie McCorkle and Thomas McGovern have spent the past year overseeing the development of their joint creation **The Barn Raising**, a **large commissioned outdoor public sculpture** for the Milton S. Hershey Medical Center in Hershey, Pa. The idea developed as a response to the farmlands which surround the center. The **artists wished to create a piece** that served as a tribute to the region's cultural heritage and to all individuals who gather together to make manifest monumental ideas. The sculpture sits on a grassy knoll in front of the entrance to the University and Children's hospitals. **It is a scaled down replica** of a standard barn structure with the back wall fixed in a tilted position, as if in the process of being raised. Outside the barn is a table made to look like wooden planks on sawhorses. Next to the table is a bench that resembles a plank on produce crates. The entire structure is **made of steel and painted red.** It is interactive; visitors may enter the barn or sit at the table. An identification sign, which normally accompanies a work of art, is incorporated into the sculpture. On top of the table, an engraved plaque replicates an architect's drawing of the barn's structure and contains the title and dedication information. McCorkle and McGovern have involved their students in the project. As a result, **these students have gained a better understanding of the complex activities that are a necessary part of any public art commission.** Their discussions have addressed the development of proposals and models, interactions with structural engineers, safety and budget issues, and the final fabrication and installation.

UNDERGRADUATE JURIED EXHIBITION

by Jim Lilly

The spring of **1993** saw the coming and going of another **Undergraduate Exhibition.** The exhibit, which opened on March 15th at the Zoller Gallery 101 Visual Arts Bldg., included **102 works by 82 artists.** A total of 399 works by 145 artists was submitted to be practically sculpted into a cohesive show by this year's juror John Vanco, **Director of the Erie Art Museum**, Erie, PA. Director Vanco's candor and experience can be appreciated through his jurors statement written for the events catalog. He stated "I was able relatively rapidly to select a large number of works, and then slowly chip away to reveal an exhibition which reflects the strengths of this department (and doubtless to some extent my own tastes and predjudices)." With that he went on to pick the shows prize winners **Robert Lynch** for his piece "Malcolm X II", **Malcolm Mobuto** for his work "Undoings", and **Susan Conard** for her piece "A Day at the Zoo". Honorable mentions went to Cara Judea Alhadeff, Bill Hosterman, and Brian Booth Craig. To all the artists whose works were accepted into the show, **congratulations.** To those artists who did not get into the show, I quote, " Not putting on a display, they shine forth. Not justifying themselves, they are distinguished. Not boasting, they receive recognition. Not bragging, they never falter. They do not quarrel, so no one quarrels with them. Therefore the ancients say, "**Yield and overcome.**" Is that an empty saying? Be really whole. And all things will come to you. — *Jim Lilly is a graduating senior in Graphic Design*

Time Magazine in its

16 pt   12 pt

January 4, 1993 issue, selected the book

8 pt

jacket for **The Secret History de-**

9 pt

signed by Penn State gradu-

12 pt

ates Chip Kidd and **Barbara**

10 pt

A detail from an interior article of the newsletter features the use of six sizes and two weights of Bodoni (left). Specific sizes and weights are indicated by blue dotted lines. This approach assigns a different emphasis to various words and phrases within the text. Line spacing is maximized to avoid overcrowding of the ascenders and descenders in the lower-case letters, to preserve the identity of each line, and to aid in overall readability. In this newsletter the type is meant to be seen as much as to be read. The design far exceeds the boundaries of normative typography, but for this arts newsletter the approach is legitimate. The audience and nature of a publication's content always determine the degree to which expressive typography may be practiced.

Extensive text set in 8 point Bodoni Book Italic describes the accomplishments of the faculty at Penn State University. While setting italics in large amounts often compromises readability, the generous leading found here greatly alleviates this problem.

Painter **Santa Barraza** *presented*

several lectures including "The History of the

22 pts

Development of Chicana Artists in Texas," at

the "Mixing It Up-5" conference at the University

of Colorado, in Boulder; "Traditional and

Designer:
Jennie Malcolm

Readers of the newsletter *Journeys* travel through a landscape of visual textures created by a sensitive combination of typefaces. Bembo, revived in 1929 by Stanley Morison of Monotype Corporation, stands as the primary text face. This typeface offers a treasure chest of font variations that retain consistency and harmony when combined together on the page. Complementing the gentle Bembo,

Futura Extra Bold and Poster Bodoni provide strength by punctuating the page with beefy running heads and paragraph openings.

In the design of any publication, you are faced with the task of identifying the various parts of the information and then determining how to typographically distinguish these parts for a clear hierarchy. This aids readability by "mapping" the information for the reader. Consider how this is accomplished in the article openings of *Journeys:*

The article title, set in 30-point Bembo Regular, is clearly established as the main element by virtue of its size.

Set in 12-point Bembo Italic, the subtitle forms a visual bridge between the title and the main text.

A two-line drop cap set in Futura Extra Bold clearly marks the beginning of the text.

The main text is set in 10/12 Bembo Regular. Its smaller size and lighter tone clearly place it on the third rung of the hierarchy ladder.

Desert Dreams

The Art of Maynard Dixon

Maynard Dixon is considered one of the foremost artists of the American West. *Desert Dreams: The Art of Maynard Dixon* is an extensive retrospective exhibition, organized by the Museum of Fine Arts, that features 70 oil paintings, sketches and photographs and includes poetry from this modernist painter of desert landscapes. A comprehensive book by guest curator Donald Hagerty, published by Gibbs-Smith Publishers, accompanies the exhibition.

In this issue

From the Museum of Fine Arts

GUSTAVE BAUMANN
Hands of a Craftsman, Heart of an Artist

DORIS CROSS: ReWorks

CRITICAL MASS

LAURA GILPIN
Photographs of the Southwest

Bembo has a full component of variations to choose from. This detail of the newsletter's contents page reveals a thoughtful blending of these variations. Italic and roman characters combine with capitals and small capitals, weaving the information into a unified whole. The visual compatibility of each member of the Bembo family makes this typographic tapestry possible. When working with typefaces, get to know all variants of the family. You will then be equipped to select and combine the variants for an effective as well as beautiful typographic message.

Bembo Regular consists of open characters, a medium weight, a small x-height, and a rather narrow character width which accommodates more characters per line than comparative Old Style book faces. Consider using Bembo when you desire a sturdy face and are short on space. Consistent in color, texture, and proportion, Bembo has only one quirky irregularity: the bowed strokes found in the upper-case *K* and lower-case *m* and *n.*

The newsletter's folios add impact and visual interest. Shown above at actual size, this unique configuration was created by shifting the word *page* vertically by thirty points from its baseline to appear centered on the numeral. You can achieve many different typographic effects using this technique, as illustrated by the bouncing letters to the left.

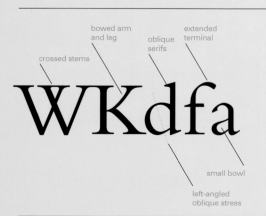

bowed arm and leg
oblique serifs
extended terminal
crossed stems
small bowl
left-angled oblique stress

WKdfa

Notice the use of white space in this publication. Contrary to uninformed opinion, this is not "wasted space." On the contrary, white space functions as a design tool to organize elements on a page, to separate units of information, and to establish a clear hierarchy between all the parts of a composition. This feature along with a balanced selection of contrasing letterforms, creates a distinctive and visually attractive newsletter.

Readers not only read the words of a text, they also experience them visually, and every typeface evokes a different response. Consider the three text settings to the right. Though each text block contains the same words, each is perceived quite differently. The top example, set in Bembo Regular, is a detail of text from the newsletter. Does the experience of reading this text differ from the that of reading Franklin Gothic (middle) or Frutiger Bold (bottom)?

At a time when solid-waste disposal has become an official focus of national and international concern, this exhibition will expose Western audiences to a largely unrecognized type of waste recy-

At a time when solid-waste disposal has become an official focus of national and international concern, this exhibition will expose Western audiences to a largely unrecognized type of waste

At a time when solid-waste disposal has become an official focus of national and international concern, this exhibition will expose Western audiences to a largely unrecognized type of waste recycling that

Designer:
Craig Minor
Cheryl Brzezinski-
Beckett

The newsletter for Innova, a Houston-based organization that provides information and programs for interior design and architecture firms, balances the splendor of colorful graphic shapes, bold images, and an energetic layout with highly readable text type-settings. In keeping with Innova's focus, the newsletter's visual organization suggests interior spaces and architectural settings. Century Expanded, a typeface with a narrow set width which contradicts its name, comfortably accommodates large amounts of information and handily fits into narrow column widths. This typeface, chosen for the main text of the newsletter, serves the reader well when used for continuous articles, and for more choppy settings such as schedules and lists.

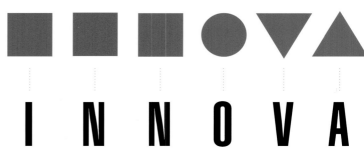

Letters comprising the title *INNOVA* in the newsletter masthead overlap the geometric shapes, circle, square, and triangle. These shapes, representing the basic building blocks in design, reflect also the inherent structure of the title letters. All letters can be reduced to these fundamental forms. The diagram above links the title letters with their corresponding shapes. The letters also overlap the shapes, appearing three-dimensional as if hovering in space.

This newsletter design appeals to the reader through an active integration of contrasting type, shapes, textures, photographs, and illustrations. Attaining diversity without sacrificing unity is a challenging goal in typography.

A 2-point rule and a geometric shape enclose a headline found on the interior of the newsletter. Similar line and shape configurations prominently display other heads within the publication. Experiment with line and picture box tools to generate your own striking type environments.

QGefd

vertical stress
low serif
round ball
oblique, slightly concave serifs
curvilinear tail
narrow set width
high contrast in strokes

Designed in 1900, Century Expanded is a crisp and highly refined typeface with a narrow set width. It has gained notoriety over the decades as a very readable and flexible text face.

Most American automobile horns
beep in the key of F.

David Louis

2201 Fascinating Facts

Interlocking shapes provide
an active environment for a
sidebar on driving safety. This
motif relates visually also to
those used for the titles and
was created with simple
shapes and lines.

For the newsletter calendar,
letters reversed from bold
black bars enable readers to
quickly find dates and events.
Other computer manipula-
tions based on this idea are
shown to the left.

One of the most important
factors in making text
readable is the amount of
space placed between the
lines. Depending on their
individual designs, typefaces
require different line
spacings. Common line
spacings are 8/10, 9/11, and
10/12, but different needs
require different adjustments.
For the best readability avoid
setting type with lines that
are too close to one another.
Crowded lines make it
difficult for the eye to move
from line to line in reading.
Each of the text blocks below
is set in 9-point Century
Expanded, a face with a large
x-height that looks best with
a couple of points of line
spacing. The examples below
consist of the newsletter's
text setting, 9/11 (top),
followed by 9/10, 9/9, and
9/8. The last example is
referred to as "negative line
spacing." This spacing is
easily generated by the
computer, but should be used
with great caution, since
obviously it is more difficult
to read than a more
normative line spacing.

This 11" x 17" newsletter is
printed in three colors
throughout. It is organized
with the aid of a four-column
grid. The main text is set
flush-left, ragged-right, but
some articles feature
centered text and images
similar to the one on driving
safety shown in this example.

Most of us get behind the wheel of a
car feeling absolutely certain that we
are cautious drivers who know the
rules of the road. We drive with confi-
dence, even bravado, assuming that we
can recognize hazards, understand

Most of us get behind the wheel of a
car feeling absolutely certain that we
are cautious drivers who know the
rules of the road. We drive with confi-
dence, even bravado, assuming that we
can recognize hazards, understand

Most of us get behind the wheel of a
car feeling absolutely certain that we
are cautious drivers who know the
rules of the road. We drive with confi-
dence, even bravado, assuming that we
can recognize hazards, understand

Most of us get behind the wheel of a
car feeling absolutely certain that we
are cautious drivers who know the
rules of the road. We drive with confi-
dence, even bravado, assuming that we
can recognize hazards, understand

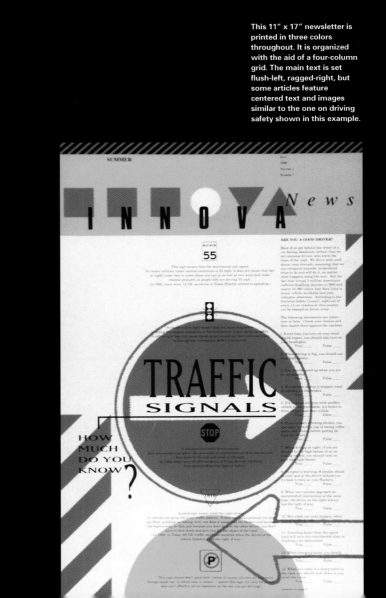

Designer:
Debbie Shmerler

The Appalachian Trail Club is an active hiking club based in Virginia. The club's newsletter, *the potomac appalachian,* is published monthly and sent to all members. Presented here is a prototype for a new design of the publication. It is inspired by the energy of the members and the scenic beauty and wonders of the trail. Upon reading the newsletter, the typography visually suggests themes associated with hiking and backpacking: steep and twisted trails, pure mountain streams, dotted lines referring to topographical maps. Each story provides a new "outdoor" experience, and yet there is never a danger of being lost; the consistent use of text type and a flexible interpretation of a grid keeps the reader on course.

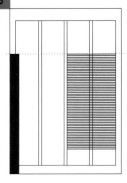

The diagram above represents the grid used for *the potomac appalachian,* and its specific use for the cover. Comprised of 4 columns, it facilitates the setting of highly readable text. The blue line indicates the horizontal alignment of the title and text block. The space above the line is reserved for the masthead.

The dynamic qualities associated with hiking in the mountains are expressed on the cover as an active field of vertical and diagonal elements. The forces exerted by these elements are balanced by the normal four-column grid. The visual orientation and position of type on a page, however subtle, can affect meaning. For example, the newsletter's title, rotated at 90° could suggest the steepness of a trail, and a relentless upward trudge.

the potomac appalachian

the newsletter of the potomac appalachian trail club, vol. 29, no. 11 november 1994

118 park street, s.e.
vienna, va 22180
703-242-0315

PATC's hike leader policy

This is your unlucky day. You agreed to lead a hike in a remote section of Shenandoah National Park, and now, climbing down a poorly maintained trail along a rocky stream bed, a hiker has caught her foot between two rocks and fallen over on her side. Her ankle is at a crazy angle, and she is in a good deal of pain. Not only that, but in the fall she tore her arm on a jagged rock and is loosing some blood. It must be seven miles at least to the next Trail head, and then a ten-mile drive to the nearest town, where you hope to find a pay phone. But it might not do much good, because you don't know who to call, anyway.
So what do you do now?

Fortunately, you have brought with you your brand new PATC Hike Leader Guide. Following its advice you brought a first aid kit, so you have something for bleeding. Moreover, it contains some emergency telephone numbers, so when you find the telephone, you can summon help.

The club has needed such a guide for some time, and the Council has adopted a policy statement on the hike leading its July 1994 meeting. The new policy is contained in the Guide, which is being handed out to all hikers.

First, the goals. PATC sponsors hikes in order to promote the enjoyment of nature. This is pretty simple stuff, but from this brief goal stems our hiking policies. Very simply, we do not want to weigh our hiking program down with alot to regulations. We do not certify hike leader nor do we require classroom instruction. We don't have a master hiking plan to which all hikes must conform.

We lead all kinds of hikes for all kinds of people. These range form short and level mid-week hikes to tough weekend conditioners, and everything in between. We promote overnight backpacking, and we also sponsor excursions to remote places.

But every hike and every leader conforms to certain established minimums. Although some are new policy statements, all are common sense. Here they are:

1 The leader must know the trail. Be sure you have hiked the trail before, and that you are familiar with current trail conditions. PATC will not sponsor events in which the leader plans on striking off into uncharted ground. And in addition to knowing the trail, know all the ancillary things - the trail head, the parking conditions, how long the hike will take, where you will have lunch, and so on.

2 The hike must be advertised in the Forecast section of the Potomac Appalachian. This doesn't foreclose any of the numerous informal groups that get together and go out on a moments notice. It does mean that these last minute hikes are not club sponsored. We try to encourage planning far enough in advance so that others can read about the hike, make room for it in their schedules, and sign up. It is only fair to the club members and non-members alike that they have plenty of opportunities to hike, without having to "know someone". If you are a leader, try to plan far enough in advance that everyone has an equal opportunity to go with you. (This is how most of the PATC work trips are handled too.)

3 Provide enough information in the Forecast ad. In addition to date, location, and so on, the ad should specify the length of the hike and the general difficulty (easy, moderate, difficult, very strenuous). This is very subjective judgment, but you can reduce the uncertainty by studying the elevation changes on the PATC trail map and by estimating your expected speed. Including "breather" stops, a standard pace is about two miles per hour. Slower than that is an easy pace and faster can be generally considered difficult or very strenuous. If you will be on very rough terrain, or if you have significant elevation changes, adjust your estimated difficulty accordingly.

4 Inform people who call you to sign up for the hike where and when you'll meet, where the trail head is, what time you will be leaving the trail head, how transportation is to be arranged, and what to bring to the hike. If you suspect that the caller is not prepared for the pace or difficulty of the terrain, question him or her closely. The final decision on who goes on the hike is yours and yours alone.

continued on page 3

Upcoming Events

Annual North District Trails Workshop
See Forecast, page 5; see story page 3.

Natural Sciences Hikes
Saturday-Monday, September 3-5, in the Three Ridges area of the Pedlar District just south of Waynesboro, and Saturday-Monday, October 8-10, in the George Washington National Forest. See Forecast, pages 4 and 7.

11th Annual Pig Roast
Saturday, October 29, at Blackburn Trail Center
See story and registration form, page 3, and forecast, page 8.

Virginia '95
PATC hosts the 30th Appalachian Trail Conference, June 30 - July 7, 1905, at James Madison University, Harrisonburg, VA. A fundraiser is urgently needed for the conference. See next page.

SNP Overseers Picnic
Attention all SNP overseers and managers: SNP appreciation picnic deadline is September 5! See box, page 11.

The title is painstakingly tracked and kerned to provide a well-spaced typographic unit (below). Compare the two settings of the word *appalachian*. The version on the left reflects the actual title. It is kerned between the awkward character pairs *pp* and *ch*. Without kerning, these characters have too much space between them in relation to the other characters. On the right the same word, void of these refinements, is shown for comparison. Always make adjustments in the letter spacing of display type, however subtle. It can mean the difference between typographic excellence and mediocrity. Be aware that every font possesses unique tracking and kerning requirements, and that your skilled judgment alone determines the need for adjustment.

The primary text is set in Caslon Regular. To provide emphasis and to invite the reader into each story, the lead sentence or phrase in the first line of type are set in Caslon Bold (top). This and similar devices provide clear signposts for article or story openings. Other variations are plentiful, a few of which are illustrated.

This is your unlucky day. You agreed to lead a hike in a remote section of Shenandoah National Park, and now, climbing down a poorly maintained trail along a rocky stream bed, a hiker has caught her foot between two rocks and fallen over on her side. Her ankle is at a crazy angle, and she is in a good deal

This is your unlucky day. **You agreed to lead a hike in a remote section of Shenandoah National Park, and now, climbing down a poorly maintained trail along a rocky stream bed, a hiker has caught her foot between two rocks and fallen over on her side. Her ankle is at a crazy angle, and she is in a good deal**

This is your unlucky day. You agreed to lead a hike in a remote section of Shenandoah National Park, and now, climbing down a poorly maintained trail along a rocky stream bed, a hiker has caught her foot between two rocks and fallen over on her side. Her ankle is at a crazy angle, and she is in a good deal

This is your unlucky day. You agreed to lead a hike in a remote section of Shenandoah National Park, and now, climbing down a poorly maintained trail along a rocky stream bed, a hiker has caught her foot between two rocks and fallen over on her side. Her ankle is at a crazy angle, and she is in a good deal

This is your unlucky day. You agreed to lead a hike in a remote section of Shenandoah National Park, and now, climbing down a poorly maintained trail along a rocky stream bed, a hiker has caught her foot between two rocks and fallen over on her side. Her ankle is at a crazy angle, and she is in a good deal

appalachian ← appalachian ←

The series of triangular forms cascading along the top of the cover reflects the mountainous terrain of the trail. This motif is a permanent part of the masthead, appearing in every issue. Notice the larger negative shape in the foreground (the white triangular shape), an expression of a snow-capped peak. The simplicity of these forms and their controlled arrangement in the space provide a sophisticated, nonliteral expression of a mountain range. These basic shapes resemble the elemental qualities earmarking Helvetica, the typeface used in the title.

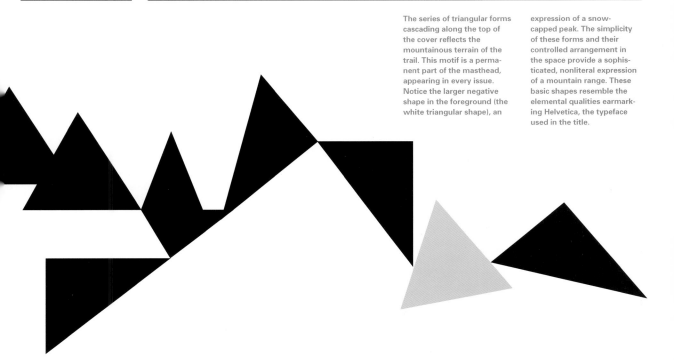

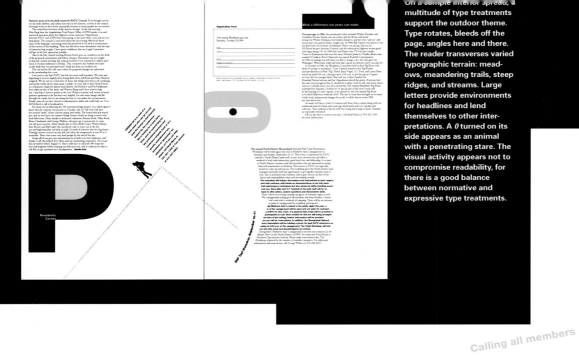

On a sample interior spread, a multitude of type treatments support the outdoor theme. Type rotates, bleeds off the page, angles here and there. The reader transverses varied typographic terrain: meadows, meandering trails, steep ridges, and streams. Large letters provide environments for headlines and lend themselves to other interpretations. A *0* turned on its side appears as an animal with a penetrating stare. The visual activity appears not to compromise readability, for there is a good balance between normative and expressive type treatments.

Text columns often stray from conventions by assuming unusual shapes. The example shown opposite was created by making an oval shape with an ellipse tool, and running text around it. Paragraphs are distinguished from one another by alternately setting them in two different typefaces of contrasting value and texture: Caslon and Helvetica Heavy.

Dotted lines, such as those representing trails on topographical maps, link newsletter components and keep the reader on course.

Calling all members   If you know of s

The annual North District Shenandoah National Park Trail Maintenance Workshop will be held again this year at Mathews Arm Campground on Saturday and Sunday, September 10-11. This event, co-sponsored by PATC and the a North District park staff, is now in its seventh year and offers a weekend of trail work instruction, good food, fun, and fellowship. Is is open to North District overseers and club members who are interested in seeing what trail maintenance is all about. Newcomers to PATC are especially invited to come up and join us. The workshop gives the North District trail managers and park staff and opportunity to get together and play host to new, old, or potential trail overseers, and to give novices an idea of the duties and responsibilities that trail stewardship entails.

The workshop will feature discussions and instructions by park rangers and club veterans, with hands-on demonstrations of not only basic trail maintenance techniques but also advanced skills including power tool use. Steve Bair and C.T. Cambell of the park staff will be on hand to offer advice, answer questions and demonstrate skills.

There will be an evening campfire program on Saturday night as well. The campground setting gives all members and their families a chance to mix trail work with a weekend of camping. There will be no entrance fee to the park or campground for workshop participants.

Although Mathews Arm is closed to the public again this year, a portion of the campground will be open and set aside for exclusive use by PATC for this event. It is planned that meals will be provided to the participants at cost. Since details for this are still being arranged at the time of the writing, further information will be provided when you call for reservations. In addition, the Shenandoah Natural History Association will be holding a picnic for park PATC volunteers on Sunday at 2:00 p.m. at the campground. The Trails Workshop will fold over into this event and all participants are invited.

Getting there: Mathews Arm Campground is located near milepost 22 off Skyline Drive in the North District of SNP. Use either the Front Royal or Thornton Gap entrance stations. Please make reservations early. The Workshop is limited by the number of available campsites. For additional information and reservations, call George Walters at 410-296-8553.

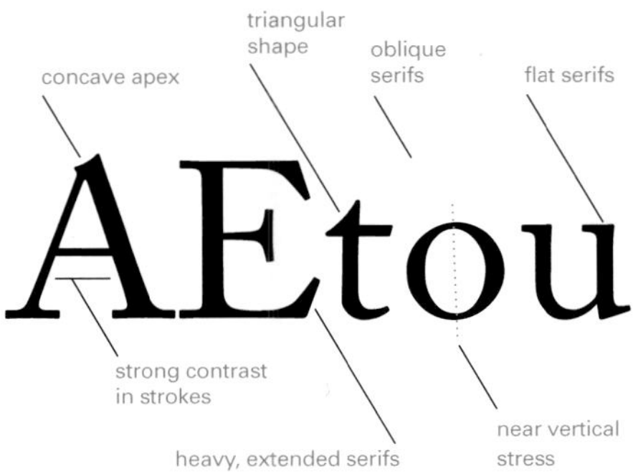

concave apex

triangular shape

oblique serifs

flat serifs

AEtou

strong contrast in strokes

heavy, extended serifs

near vertical stress

Caslon types were first designed by William Caslon in 1725. Though individually some Caslon characters lack refined proportions, set together as text they possess a vigorous texture and excellent legibility. The long-lived Caslon fonts remain a favorite choice among contemporary book and magazine designers.

...ing in hiking, hunting, or sporting equipment, or any other retailers who might sell our maps and books, please send a note to Patricia Fankhauser, PATC sales coordinator. She'll contact the store, provide samples, and explain the sales terms.

In an announcement to members, a high-contrast image of a hiker descends a peak composed of two long lines of text type juxtaposed at a 90° angle. Type and image join to tell a story. The words *Calling all members,* assigned a color of gold/yellow, direct the reader to the beginning of the announcement.

President's Corner

When letters are enlarged and manipulated in an unexpected manner, they acquire a visual presence, demanding to be seen and recognized as well as read. The counter of a Helvetica Heavy *P,* normally seen as the same color as the background of the letter, thwarts reader expectations by appearing as yellow (left).

Positioned within the imposing letter P is the headline, *President's Corner.* The headline type, set flush-right, ragged left, is positioned precisely at a corner of the letter, establishing an amusing double meaning.

The yellow counter within the capital *P* was achieved by creating a square shape slightly larger than the counter, filling it with yellow, positioning it over the counter, and then "sending it to the back."

Designer:
Terry Veit

It is reasonable and perhaps expected that the *Alumni Newsletter* for the Department of Communication Arts and Design at Virginia Commonwealth University should feature experimental, even outrageous typography. Although the newsletter is printed in only one color, typography and images emblazon its pages with vivid texture and a carnival of effects. Type appears to explode on one page, while on another it establishes a playful, sculptural environment. If type is capable of functioning as the visual equivalent of conversation, then in this newsletter the reader experiences all of the discourse, laughter, emotion, and babble inherent in each page.

The vibrating newsletter cover features type that appears to weave in and out of a framework of bold stripes. When text type falls on a black stripe, it appears as white, and when it falls on a white stripe, it appears as black. The stripes, combined with a four-column grid, provide an organizational framework for the design. A series of four squares, centrally located on the page, provide "windows" for the placement of images and text. These squares may be observed in many variations throughout the pages.

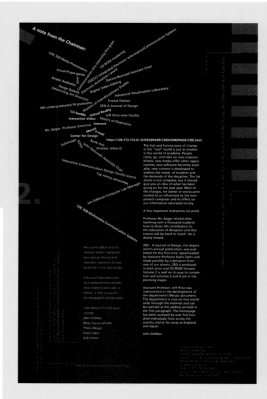

As the Fall 94 term progresses, three
position. Committees composed of fa
and sifting through numerous a
of applicants. Faculty candidates are
and familiarization. One candidate is
at the administrative level. **D**ue to the
needed to teach courses and develop

Nic arrived in Richmond in 1962 from Syracuse, New York, where he received his MFA degree in painting from Syracuse University. Prior to coming to Richmond, he worked as a medical illustrator, and during his early training as an studied with several prominent figures, including Josef Albers, Fletcher Martin (the illustrating cowboy), and Bouche. He studied fresco painting with Jean Charlot. Among his peers, Nic is known and respected as one of

The newsletter for the Chicago Chapter of the American Institute of Graphic Arts provides an excellent case study of typography devoted not only to readability, but also to the flair and drama of visual contrast. It is more of an understatement than overstatement, however, and it is obviously committed to function rather than style. Lying on a table among high-gloss, four-color printed ephemera, the newsletter resonates and stands apart with bold forms printed in black ink on white paper. What makes the publication visually distinct is the absence of color rather than the presence of it. It is a visually refined and sophisticated publication, one responsive to its audience of graphic arts practitioners. Bodoni Book, readable and classic in character, is used for the text. Article titles and heads are set in Univers 85 for its dark tone and visual weight.

What makes the covers of *CHICAIGAO* so engaging, so visually enticing? Several factors, including the prominent, centered masthead, which ingeniously combines the acronym *AIGA*, (American Institute of Graphic Arts) with the word *CHICAGO*. Since both elements share the same letters, they are capable of being read simultaneously. Also, vivid black and white line illustrations anchored at the bottoms of the covers provide visual narratives about the newsletter's contents. Two ruled lines, one thick and the other thin, divide the space into two information zones. The top zone identifies the AIGA Chicago Chapter; the second zone reveals the contents of the specific issue.

Integrated into this clean, contemporary-looking design are traditional versals, or initial capitals that mark the beginning of text. Borrowed from scribal practice during the Medieval period, versals can be used in a great many ways, from familiar drop caps and raised caps to more eccentric and outlandish deviations. You may use for versals the same typeface as used in the text, or choose a contrasting face for a more pronounced statement. Most page-layout programs provide tools for making drop caps within text. But versals can also be created separately and inserted as desired into the text.

The creation and management of Mobium Corporation for Design and Communication raised a number of crucial issues that may prove illuminating for design professionals.

Mobium was founded in 1979 by uniting management and design resources of Unimark International with the Creative Services Department of R.R. Donnelley & Sons Co.

Within text, paragraphs can be indicated in a myriad of ways. In this newsletter, a basic 1.5-pica indent is used. But other methods are plentiful, depending upon your specific design. A few possibilities are explored in the examples to the right.

The creation and management of Mobium Corporation for Design and Communication raised a number of crucial issues that may prove illuminating for design professionals.

was founded in 1979 by uniting management and design resources of Unimark International with the Creative Services Department of R.R. Donnelley & Sons Co.

The creation and management of Mobium Corporation for Design and Communication raised a number of crucial issues that may prove illuminating for design professionsls. Mobium was founded in 1979 by uniting management and design resources of Unimark International with the Creative Services Department of R.R. Donnelley & Sons Co.

The creation and management of Mobium Corporation for Design and Communication raised a number of crucial issues that may prove illuminating for design professionals. Mobium was founded in 1979 by uniting management and design resources of Unimark International with the Creative Services Department of R.R. Donnelley & Sons Co.

The creation and management of Mobium Corporation for Design and Communication raised a number of crucial issues that may prove illuminating for design professionals. ■ Mobium was founded in 1979 by uniting management and design resources of Unimark International with the Creative Services Department of R.R. Donnelley & Sons Co.

These 11" x 17" pages are organized with the aid of a three-column grid consisting of very narrow margins: 2 picas at top and sides, and 3.5 picas at the bottom. The text columns measure 20 picas and are separated with a 1-pica interval. A horizontal flow line begins 11 picas from the top of the page. This structure gives the publication a very full look, and indeed it is packed with information. But the way in which the text is handled prevents it from appearing too crowded. The text is set in 12/14 Bodoni Book, flush-left, ragged right. Article titles, positioned at the tops of pages, consist of 15/18 Univers 85, and author names are set in 18/18 Bodoni Book to match the size of the titles.

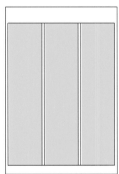

An important factor contributing to the clarity and readability of this newsletter is the restrained use of different type faces and sizes. Titles, names of authors, text, and subheads are consistent from article to article, and as few parameters as possible distinguish these elements. For example, titles and author names are set in different typefaces, but appear as the same size. The same conditions hold true for the subheads and text. Generally, too many uncontrolled type sizes and styles on a page can confuse readers. A good way to think about distinguishing typographic parts is to make them similar as well as different in some respect. The top example is similar in size but different in typeface. The bottom example possesses no similarity among parts.

Managing a Multi-Office Design Firm
Ron Kovach

Managing a Multi-Office Design Firm
RON KOVACH

Page 14–15
Credits for paintings reproduced on covers of *A History of Western Society* are as follows:

Volume A: *Portrait of an Egyptian,* detail. Greco-Roman Egyptian, 3rd c. A.D. J. Paul Getty Museum, Malibu, California. Werner Forman/Art Resource, New York.

Volume B: Marinus van Remerswaele. *The Tax Collector of Money Changer,* c 1540. Musee des Beaux-Arts, Valenciennes, France. Erich Lessing/Art Resource, New York.

Volume C: Carl Olaf Larson. *Self-Portrait.* Uffizi, Florence, Italy. Scala/Art Resources, New York.

Volume I: Hans Memling. *Man with a Coin,* 15th c. Koninklijk Museum voor Schone Kunsten, Plaatnijdersstraat 2-B-2000, Antwerp, Belgium.

Since 1400: Sir Joshua Reynolds. *Portrait Study.* Kunsthistorisches Museum, Vienna, Austria. Nimatallah/Art Resource, New York.

Page 112
The photograph of fireworks on the cover of the January-February issue © Akira Inoue, Photonica; the Mr. Rogers still on the March–April cover © 1985, 1986 Family Communications, Inc.

Page 113
The Mr. Rogers still © 1985, 1986 Family Communications, Inc.; the photograph for the "Body as Music" © Howard Schatz, Photonica; photograph of Enzenberger © Ted Russell; photograph of Kapuściński © Czeslaw Czaplinski; art for January–February spreads by Andrew Henderson.

Pages 136–137
Newsletter design courtesy of Harold Burch, Pentagram Design.

Reproductions of design throughout the book courtesy of featured designers.

Publication designs on pages 54–57, 88-91, 128-131, and 146-149 are prototypes and are not available for distribution.

The quotation used periodically in type specimens is from *The Alphabet and Elements of Lettering* by Frederic W. Goudy, courtesy of Dover Publications, Inc., New York, New York.

Sources for fonts

Adobe Systems, Incorporated
P.O. Box 6458
Salinas, California 93912-6458

1 800 64-ADOBE

Bitstream Inc.
215 First Street
Cambridge, Massachusetts 02142

1 800 237 3335

Carter & Cone Type, Inc.
2155 Massachusetts Avenue
Cambridge, Massachusetts 02140

1 617 876 5447

Emigré
4475 D Street
Sacramento, California 95819

1 800 944 9021

FontHaus, Inc.
1375 Kings Highway East
Fairfield, Connecticut 06430

203 367 1993

Linotype-Hell Company
425 Oser Avenue
Hauppauge, New York 11788

1 800 633 1900

Monotype Typography, Inc.
Suite 504
53 West Jackson Boulevard
Chicago, Illinois 60604

1 800 MONOTYPE

Gail Anderson
Lee Bearson
Debra Bishop
Geraldine Hessler
Eric Siry
Fred Woodward
Rolling Stone Magazine
1290 6th Avenue
New York, New York 10104

Frank Armstrong
Armstrong Design Consultants
P.O. Box 12234
Research Triangle Park
North Carolina 27709-2234

Roger E. Baer
College of Design
Iowa State University
Ames, Iowa 50011

Banu Berker
Banu Berker Graphic Design
15 Third Place
Brooklyn, New York 11231

Cheryl Brzezinski-Beckett
Craig Minor
Minor Design Group
1973 West Gray, Suite 22
Houston, Texas 77019

Anne Bush
Karen White
Department of Art
2525 The Mall
University of Hawaii at Manoa
Honolulu, Hawaii 96822

Harold Burch
Harold Burch Design
126 Fifth Avenue, 15th floor
New York, New York 10011

Chuck Byrne
Chuck Byrne Design
5528 Lawton Avenue
Oakland, California 94618-1509

Ronn Campisi
Ronn Campisi Design
118 Newbury Street
Boston, Massachusetts 02116

Rob Carter
Communication Arts and Design
School of the Arts
Virginia Commonwealth
University
P.O. Box 842519
Richmond, Virginia 23284-2519

Larry G. Clarkson
Clarkson Creative
1472 South 800 East
Salt Lake City, Utah 84107

David Colley
Communication Arts and Design
School of the Arts
Virginia Commonwealth
University
P.O. Box 842519
Richmond, Virginia 23284-2519

Ned Drew
Visual and Performing Arts
110 Warren Street
Bradley Hall, Room 520
Rutgers University
Newark, New Jersey 07102

Detlef Fiedler
Daniela Haufe
Cyan
Rosenthaler Strasse 13
10119 Berlin, Germany

Barbara Glauber
Heavy Meta
596 Broadway, Suite 1212
New York, New York 10012

Diana Graham
Cody Rasmussen
Diagram
22 West 19 Street, 9th floor
New York, New York 10011

April Greiman
April Greiman Associates
620 Moulton Avenue #211
Los Angeles, California 90031

Andrew Henderson
Utne Reader
1624 Harmon Place
Minneapolis, Minnesota 55403

Ken Hiebert
7731 Mill Road
Elkins Park, Pennsylvania
19027-2708

Jerry Hutchinson
Hutchinson Associates, Inc.
1147 West Ohio, Suite 305
Chicago, Illinois 60622

Mirko Ilić
652 Hudson Street #3W
New York, New York 10014

Jan Jancourt
Minneapolis College
of Art and Design
2501 Stevens Avenue South
Minneapolis, Minnesota 55404

Polly Johnson
Graphic Design Department
Ringling School of Art and Design
2700 North Tamiami Trail
Sarasota, Florida 34234-5895

Somi Kim
Reverb
5514 Wilshire Blvd. #900
Los Angeles, California 90036

Willi Kunz
Willi Kunz Associates, Inc.
2112 Broadway
New York, New York 10023

Brian Lane
Henry Vizcarra
30sixty design, inc.
2801 Cahuenga Blvd. West
Los Angeles, California 90068

Jenny Malcolm
Malcolm Design
709 West Johnson Street
Suite 204
Raleigh, North Carolina 27603

John Malinoski
5
4204 Springhill Avenue
Richmond, Virginia 23225

Peter Martin
Amy Puglisi
Debbie Shmerler
Terry Veit
Communication Arts and Design
School of the Arts
Virginia Commonwealth
University
P.O. Box 842519
Richmond, Virginia 23284-2519

Takaaki Matsumoto
Matsumoto Incorporated
17 Cornelia Street
New York, New York 10014

Philip B. Meggs
Communication Arts and Design
School of the Arts
Virginia Commonwealth
University
P.O. Box 842519
Richmond, Virginia 23284-2519

Jennifer Morla
Morla Design
463 Bryant Street
San Francisco, California 94107

Aleš Najbrt
Raut
Bolívarova 23
169 00 Praha 6
Czech Republic

Christopher Ozubko
Studio Ozubko
3044 38th Avenue West
Seattle, Washington 98199

Katie Salen
Barbara Foley
Sonya Mead
Center for Design Studies
School of the Arts
Virginia Commonwealth
University
P.O. Box 842519
Richmond, Virginia 23284-2519

Paula Scher
Pentagram Design
212 Fifth Avenue
New York, Nw York 10010

Kristin Breslin Sommese
Lanny Sommese
Brett M. Critchlow
Scott Patt
Jim Lilly
Sommese Design
481 Glenn Road
State College, Pennsylvania 16803

Robert Wiser
Archetype Press
4201 Connecticut Avenue NW
Suite 407
Washington, DC 20008

Carl Wohlt
Crosby Associates, Inc.
676 St. Clair
Chicago, Illinois 60611

Matt Woolman
Fusion
3110 Park Avenue #1
Richmond, Virginia 23221

Items appearing in blue are concepts specifically related to working with type.

Typefaces are identified in *italics*

During the process of writing and designing this book, several people generously provided help, criticism, and advice. To them I extend my special thanks. The book could not be realized without the generous support of the contributing designers whose work appears throughout the pages. Diana Lively copy edited the book; her attention to detail is greatly appreciated. My daughter, Mindy Carter, a student at the University of Virginia, read the manuscript, provided suggestions, and compiled the index. Thomas J. Stallings provided much needed help and advice during the early phases of the project. My colleagues, Philip Meggs and John Malinoski responded to frequent questions, and criticized content and design. I thank them for their friendship, intelligence, and professionalism. Sandy Wheeler reviewed the manuscript, provided insight, and kept me "on belay" always. Jerry Bates and Jeff Price provided invaluable technical help. Matt Woolman designed many of the book's pages, and offered generous assistance during all phases of the project. Maria Rogal enthusiastically shared resources that greatly affected the content of the book. At Virginia Commonwealth University, Dr. Murry N. DePillars and John DeMao offered continued support. Sally Carter, my wife, offered unending encouragement and extraordinarily good humor during months of intense preparation.

Working with Computer Type was typeset and designed in QuarkXPress on a Power Macintosh 7100/66. Text throughout the book is set in the Univers family.

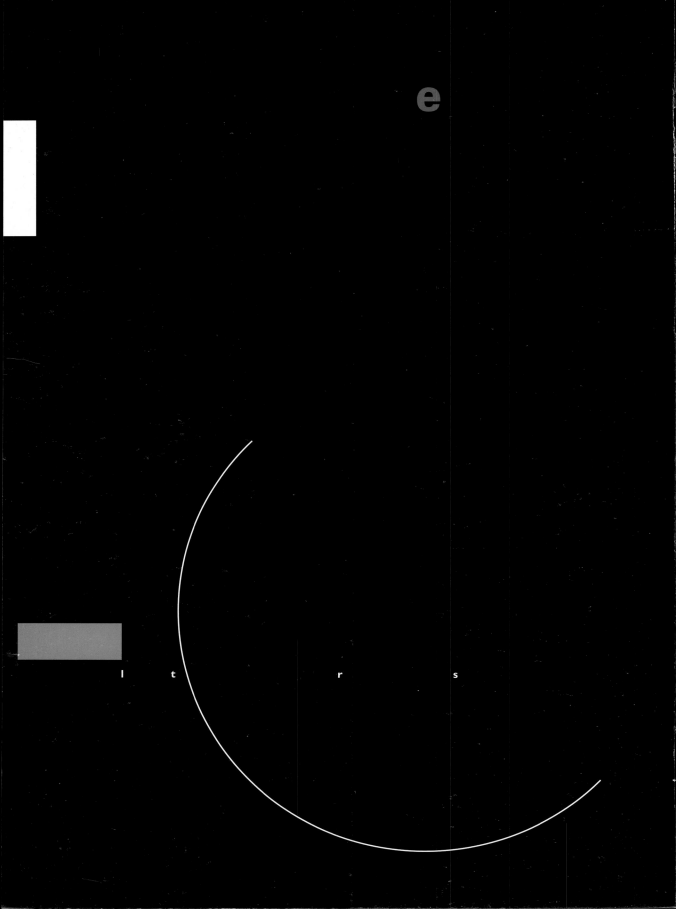